Riverby Edition

THE WRITINGS OF
JOHN BURROUGHS

WITH PORTRAITS AND MANY ILLUSTRATIONS

VOLUME XV

John Burroughs

THE WRITINGS

OF

JOHN BURROUGHS

XV

LEAF AND TENDRIL

BOSTON AND NEW YORK

HOUGHTON MIFFLIN COMPANY

The Riverside Press Cambridge

PREFACE

As most of the essays in this volume were written in a little bark-covered study that is surrounded on all sides by vineyards, I have thought it not inappropriate for me to go to the vine for a title for the collection. The "leaf" may stand very well for the nature sketches, and the "tendril" may symbolize those other papers in which I have groped my way in some of the great problems, seeking some law or truth to cling to. The tendril is blind, but it is sensitive and outreaching, and aided by the wind, never ceases to feel this way and that for support. Whatever it touches it clings to. One vine will cling to another, or one arm cling to another arm of the same vine. It has no power to select or discriminate — its one overmastering impulse is to cling, no matter to what. Where the tendril strikes the wire, or hooks that sensitive finger around it, how quickly it tightens its hold and winds itself round and round! In time it becomes almost as hard as the wire itself.

I, too, have groped my way more or less blindly in some of the great questions that confront us in this world vineyard, and have clung to what I could find, maybe sometimes only to my own conceits or vague vaticinations.

The vines have other hints for me which I try to

PREFACE

profit by. In the mild winter days, while I am writing in my cabin study, I can hear the sharp "click, click" of Hud's shears as he trims the vines. If I could only trim my vines as heroically as Hud trims his! getting rid of all the old wood possible and leaving only a few young and vigorous shoots. The great art of grape-growing is severe trimming and high culture, and I suspect the art of literature is about the same. In the vineyard it is not foliage and wood that we are after, but grapes, and in literature verbiage and superfluities are to be kept down for the same reason — we want fruit. We have to discipline the vines severely; no riotous living, no kicking up their heels along the wires, the push of their whole life going to wood instead of grapes. At a certain time we pinch or clip the ends of all the fruit-bearing canes, cut the tendrils from the wires, chasten and humble them, and make them pause and consider. And they consider very well, for in a day or two the fruit-bunches swell perceptibly. Then later, in July, we scissor off all extra bunches, covering the ground with them, and so send the whole force of the vine into those that remain.

This is the gospel of the vine-dresser, and I would I could always make it mine when I write my essays.

January, 1908.

CONTENTS

The frontispiece portrait of Mr. Burroughs is from a photograph taken in 1905.

LIST OF ILLUSTRATIONS

LEAF AND TENDRIL

I

THE ART OF SEEING THINGS

i

I DO not purpose to attempt to tell my reader how to see things, but only to talk about the art of seeing things, as one might talk of any other art. One might discourse about the art of poetry, or of painting, or of oratory, without any hope of making one's readers or hearers poets or painters or orators.

The science of anything may be taught or acquired by study; the art of it comes by practice or inspiration. The art of seeing things is not something that may be conveyed in rules and precepts; it is a matter vital in the eye and ear, yea, in the mind and soul, of which these are the organs. I have as little hope of being able to tell the reader how to see things as I would have in trying to tell him how to fall in love or to enjoy his dinner. Either he does or he does not, and that is about all there is of it. Some people seem born with eyes in their heads, and others with buttons or painted marbles, and no amount of science can make the one equal to the other in the art of seeing things. The great mass of mankind are, in this respect, like the rank and file of an army: they fire vaguely in the direction of the enemy, and if they hit, it is more a matter of chance than of accurate aim. But here and there is the keen-eyed observer; he is the sharpshooter; his eye selects and discriminates, his purpose goes to the mark.

Even the successful angler seems born, and not made; he appears to know instinctively the ways of trout. The secret is, no doubt, love of the sport. Love sharpens the eye, the ear, the touch; it quickens the feet, it steadies the hand, it arms against the wet and the cold. What we love to do, that we do well. To know is not all; it is only half. To love is the other half. Wordsworth's poet was contented if he might enjoy the things which others understood. This is generally the attitude of the young and of the poetic nature. The man of science, on the other hand, is contented if he may understand the things that others enjoy: that is his enjoyment. Contemplation and absorption for the one; investigation and classification for the other. We probably all have, in varying degrees, one or the other of these ways of enjoying Nature: either the sympathetic and emotional enjoyment of her which the young and the artistic and the poetic temperament have, or the enjoyment through our knowing faculties afforded by natural science, or, it

The Angler

may be, the two combined, as they certainly were in such a man as Tyndall.

But nothing can take the place of love. Love is the measure of life: only so far as we love do we really live. The variety of our interests, the width of our sympathies, the susceptibilities of our hearts — if these do not measure our lives, what does? As the years go by, we are all of us more or less subject to two dangers, the danger of petrifaction and the danger of putrefaction; either that we shall become hard and callous, crusted over with customs and conventions till no new ray of light or of joy can reach us, or that we shall become lax and disorganized, losing our grip upon the real and vital sources of happiness and power. Now, there is no preservative and antiseptic, nothing that keeps one's heart young, like love, like sympathy, like giving one's self with enthusiasm to some worthy thing or cause.

If I were to name the three most precious resources of life, I should say books, friends, and nature; and the greatest of these, at least the most constant and always at hand, is nature. Nature we have always with us, an inexhaustible storehouse of that which moves the heart, appeals to the mind, and fires the imagination, — health to the body, a stimulus to the intellect, and joy to the soul. To the scientist Nature is a storehouse of facts, laws, processes; to the artist she is a storehouse of pictures; to the poet she is a storehouse of images, fancies, a source of inspiration; to the moralist she is a storehouse of precepts and parables; to all she may be a source of knowledge and joy.

II

There is nothing in which people differ more than in their powers of observation. Some are only half alive to what is going on around them. Others, again, are keenly alive: their intelligence, their powers of recognition, are in full force in eye and ear at all times. They see and hear everything, whether it directly concerns them or not. They never pass unseen a familiar face on the street; they are never oblivious of any interesting feature or sound or object in the earth or sky about them. Their power of attention is always on the alert, not by conscious effort, but by natural habit and disposition. Their perceptive faculties may be said to be always on duty. They turn to the outward world a more highly sensitized mind than other people. The things that pass before them are caught and individualized instantly. If they visit new countries, they see the characteristic features of the people and scenery at once. The impression is never blurred or confused. Their powers of observation suggest the sight and scent of wild animals; only, whereas it is fear that sharpens the one, it is love and curiosity that sharpens the other. The mother turkey with her brood sees the hawk when it is a mere speck against the sky; she is, in her solicitude for her young, thinking of hawks, and is on her guard against them. Fear makes keen her eye. The hunter does not see the hawk till his attention is thus called to it by the turkey, because his interests are not endangered; but he outsees the wild creatures of the plain and mountain, — the elk, the antelope, and the mountain-sheep, — he makes it his business to look for them, and his eyes carry farther than do theirs.

We may see coarsely and vaguely, as most people do, noting only masses and unusual appearances, or we may see finely and discriminatingly, taking in the minute and the specific. In a collection of stuffed birds, the other day, I observed that a wood thrush was mounted as in the act of song, its open beak pointing straight to the zenith. The taxidermist had not seen truly. The thrush sings with its beak but slightly elevated. Who has not seen a red squirrel or a gray squirrel running up and down the trunk of a tree? But probably very few have noticed that the position of the hind feet is the reverse in the one case from what it is in the other. In descending they are extended to the rear, the toe-nails hooking to the bark, checking and controlling the fall. In most pictures the feet are shown well drawn up under the body in both cases.

5

People who discourse pleasantly and accurately about the birds and flowers and external nature generally are not invariably good observers. In their walks do they see anything they did not come out to see? Is there any spontaneous or unpremeditated seeing? Do they make discoveries? Any bird or creature may be hunted down, any nest discovered, if you lay siege to it; but to find what you are not looking for, to catch the shy winks and gestures on every side, to see all the by-play going on around you, missing no significant note or movement, penetrating every screen with your eye-beams — that is to be an observer; that is to have " an eye practiced like a blind man's touch," — a touch that can distinguish a white horse from a black, — a detective eye that reads the faintest signs. When Thoreau was at Cape Cod, he noticed that the horses there had a certain muscle in their hips inordinately developed by reason of the insecure footing in the ever-yielding sand. Thoreau's vision at times fitted things closely. During some great fête in Paris, the Empress Eugénie and Queen Victoria were both present. A reporter noticed that when the royal personages came to sit down, Eugénie looked behind her before doing so, to see that the chair was really there, but Victoria seated herself without the backward glance, knowing there must be a seat ready: there always had been, and there always would be, for her. The

6

correspondent inferred that the incident showed the difference between born royalty and hastily made royalty. I wonder how many persons in that vast assembly made this observation; probably very few. It denoted a gift for seeing things.

If our powers of observation were quick and sure enough, no doubt we should see through most of the tricks of the sleight-of-hand man. He fools us because his hand is more dexterous than our eye. He captures our attention, and then commands us to see only what he wishes us to see.

In the field of natural history, things escape us because the actors are small, and the stage is very large and more or less veiled and obstructed. The movement is quick across a background that tends to conceal rather than expose it. In the printed page the white paper plays quite as important a part as the type and the ink; but the book of nature is on a different plan: the page rarely presents a contrast of black and white, or even black and brown, but only of similar tints, gray upon gray, green upon green, or drab upon brown.

By a close observer I do not mean a minute, cold-blooded specialist, —

> " a fingering slave,
> One who would peep and botanize
> Upon his mother's grave," —

but a man who looks closely and steadily at nature, and notes the individual features of tree and rock

7

and field, and allows no subtile flavor of the night
or day, of the place and the season, to escape him.
His senses are so delicate that in his evening walk
he feels the warm and the cool streaks in the air, his
nose detects the most fugitive odors, his ears the
most furtive sounds. As he stands musing in the
April twilight, he hears that fine, elusive stir and
rustle made by the angleworms reaching out from
their holes for leaves and grasses; he hears the
whistling wings of the woodcock as it goes swiftly
by him in the dusk; he hears the call of the kill-
dee come down out of the March sky; he hears
far above him in the early morning the squeaking
cackle of the arriving blackbirds pushing north;
he hears the soft, prolonged, lulling call of the little
owl in the cedars in the early spring twilight; he
hears at night the roar of the distant waterfall, and
the rumble of the train miles across the country
when the air is "hollow;" before a storm he notes
how distant objects stand out and are brought
near on those brilliant days that we call "weather-
breeders." When the mercury is at zero or lower,
he notes how the passing trains hiss and simmer
as if the rails or wheels were red-hot. He reads the
subtile signs of the weather. The stars at night
forecast the coming day to him; the clouds at
evening and at morning are a sign. He knows there
is the wet-weather diathesis and the dry-weather
diathesis, or, as Goethe said, water affirmative

8

and water negative, and he interprets the symptoms accordingly. He is keenly alive to all outward impressions. When he descends from the hill in the autumn twilight, he notes the cooler air of the valley like a lake about him; he notes how, at other seasons, the cooler air at times settles down between the mountains like a vast body of water, as shown by the level line of the fog or the frost upon the trees.

The modern man looks at nature with an eye of sympathy and love where the earlier man looked with an eye of fear and superstition. Hence he sees more closely and accurately; science has made his eye steady and clear. To a hasty traveler through the land, the farms and country homes all seem much alike, but to the people born and reared there, what a difference! They have read the fine print that escapes the hurried eye and that is so full of meaning. Every horizon line, every curve in hill or valley, every tree and rock and spring run, every turn in the road and vista in the landscape, has its special features and makes its own impression.

Scott wrote in his journal: "Nothing is so tiresome as walking through some beautiful scene with a minute philosopher, a botanist, or a pebble-gatherer, who is eternally calling your attention from the grand features of the natural picture to look at grasses and chuckie-stanes." No doubt Scott's large, generous way of looking at things

9

kindles the imagination and touches the sentiments more than does this minute way of the specialist. The nature that Scott gives us is like the air and the water that all may absorb, while what the specialist gives us is more like some particular element or substance that only the few can appropriate. But Scott had his specialties, too, the specialties of the sportsman; he was the first to see the hare's eyes as she sat in her form, and he knew the ways of grouse and pheasants and trout. The ideal observer turns the enthusiasm of the sportsman into the channels of natural history, and brings home a finer game than ever fell to shot or bullet. He too has an eye for the fox and the rabbit and the migrating water-fowl, but he sees them with loving and not with murderous eyes.

III

So far as seeing things is an art, it is the art of keeping your eyes and ears open. The art of nature is all in the direction of concealment. The birds, the animals, all the wild creatures, for the most part try to elude your observation. The art of the bird is to hide her nest; the art of the game you are in quest of is to make itself invisible. The flower seeks to attract the bee and the moth by its color and perfume, because they are of service to it; but I presume it would hide from the excursionists and the picnickers if it could, because they extirpate it.

10

THE ART OF SEEING THINGS

Power of attention and a mind sensitive to outward objects, in these lies the secret of seeing things. Can you bring all your faculties to the front, like a house with many faces at the doors and windows; or do you live retired within yourself, shut up in your own meditations? The thinker puts all the powers of his mind in reflection: the observer puts all the powers of his mind in perception; every faculty is directed outward; the whole mind sees through the eye and hears through the ear. He has an objective turn of mind as opposed to a sub-jective. A person with the latter turn of mind sees little. If you are occupied with your own thoughts, you may go through a museum of curiosities and observe nothing.

Of course one's powers of observation may be cultivated as well as anything else. The senses of seeing and hearing may be quickened and trained as well as the sense of touch. Blind persons come to be marvelously acute in their powers of touch. Their feet find the path and keep it. They come to know the lay of the land through this sense, and recognize the roads and surfaces they have once traveled over. Helen Keller reads your speech by putting her hand upon your lips, and is thrilled by the music of an instrument through the same sense of touch. The perceptions of school-children should be trained as well as their powers of reflection and memory. A teacher in Connecticut, Miss Aiken, —

11

whose work on mind-training I commend to all teachers, — has hit upon a simple and ingenious method of doing this. She has a revolving blackboard upon which she writes various figures, numbers, words, sentences, which she exposes to the view of the class for one or two or three seconds, as the case may be, and then asks them to copy or repeat what was written. In time they become astonishingly quick, especially the girls, and can take in a multitude of things at a glance. Detectives, I am told, are trained after a similar method; a man is led quickly by a show-window, for instance, and asked to name and describe the objects he saw there. Life itself is of course more or less a school of this kind, but the power of concentrated attention in most persons needs stimulating. Here comes in the benefit of manual-training schools. To *do* a thing, to make something, the powers of the mind must be focused. A boy in building a boat will get something that all the books in the world cannot give him. The concrete, the definite, the discipline of real things, the educational values that lie here, are not enough appreciated.

IV

The book of nature is like a page written over or printed upon with different-sized characters and in many different languages, interlined and cross-lined, and with a great variety of marginal notes and references. There is coarse print and fine print; there are obscure signs and hieroglyphics. We all read the large type more or less apprecia- tively, but only the students and lovers of nature read the fine lines and the footnotes. It is a book which he reads best who goes most slowly or even tarries long by the way. He who runs may read some things. We may take in the general features of sky, plain, and river from the express train, but only the pedestrian, the saunterer, with eyes in his head and love in his heart, turns every leaf and peruses every line. One man sees only the migrat- ing water-fowls and the larger birds of the air; another sees the passing kinglets and hurrying warblers as well. For my part, my delight is to linger long over each page of this marvelous record, and to dwell fondly upon its most obscure text.

I take pleasure in noting the minute things about me. I am interested even in the ways of the wild bees, and in all the little dramas and tragedies that occur in field and wood. One June day, in my walk, as I crossed a rather dry, high-lying field, my attention was attracted by small mounds of fresh earth all over the ground, scarcely more than a handful in each. On looking closely, I saw that in the middle of each mound there was a hole not quite so large as a lead-pencil. Now, I had never observed these mounds before, and my curiosity was aroused. "Here is some fine print," I said, "that I have overlooked." So I set to work to try to read it; I waited for a sign of life. Presently I saw here and there a bee hovering about over the mounds. It looked like the honey-bee, only less pronounced in color and manner. One of them alighted on one of the mounds near me, and was about to disappear in the hole in the centre when I caught it in my hand. Though it stung me, I retained it and looked it over, and in the process was stung several times; but the pain was slight. I saw it was one of our native wild bees, cousin to the leaf-rollers, that build their nests under stones and in decayed fence-rails. (In Packard I found it described under the name of *Andrena*.) Then I inserted a small weed-stalk into one of the holes, and, with a little trowel I carried, proceeded to dig out the nest. The hole was about a foot deep; at the bottom of it I found a little semi-transparent, membranous sac or cell, a little larger than that of the honey-bee; in this sac was a little pellet of yellow pollen — a loaf of bread for the young grub when the egg should have hatched. I explored other nests and found them all the same. This discovery was not a great addition to my sum of natural knowledge, but it was something. Now when I see the signs in a field, I know what they mean: they indicate the tiny earthen cradles of *Andrena*.

Near by I chanced to spy a large hole in the turf, with no mound of soil about it. I could put the end

of my little finger into it. I peered down, and saw
the gleam of two small, bead-like eyes. I knew it to
be the den of the wolf-spider. Was she waiting for
some blundering insect to tumble in? I say she,
because the real ogre among the spiders is the female. The male is small and of little consequence.
A few days later I paused by this den again and
saw the members of the ogress scattered about her
own door. Had some insect Jack the Giant-Killer
been there, or had a still more formidable ogress,
the sand-hornet, dragged her forth and carried
away her limbless body to her den in the bank?

What the wolf-spider does with the earth it excavates in making its den is a mystery. There is no
sign of it anywhere about. Does it force its way
down by pushing the soil to one side and packing
it there firmly? The entrance to the hole usually
has a slight rim or hem to keep the edge from
crumbling in.

As it happened, I chanced upon another interesting footnote that very day. I was on my way to
a muck swamp in the woods, to see if the showy
lady's-slipper was in bloom. Just on the margin of
the swamp, in the deep shade of the hemlocks, my
eye took note of some small, unshapely creature
crawling hurriedly over the ground. I stooped
down, and saw it was some large species of moth
just out of its case, and in a great hurry to find a
suitable place in which to hang itself up and give

its wings a chance to unfold before the air dried them. I thrust a small twig in its way, which it instantly seized upon. I lifted it gently, carried it to drier ground, and fixed the stick in the fork of a tree, so that the moth hung free a few feet from the ground. Its body was distended nearly to the size of one's little finger, and surmounted by wings that were so crumpled and stubby that they seemed quite rudimentary. The creature evidently knew what it wanted, and knew the importance of haste. Instantly these rude, stubby wings began to grow. It was a slow process, but one could see the change from minute to minute. As the wings expanded, the body contracted. By some kind of pumping arrangement air was being forced from a reservoir in the one into the tubes of the other. The wings were not really growing, as they at first seemed to be, but they were unfolding and expanding under this pneumatic pressure from the body. In the course of about half an hour the process was completed, and the winged creature hung there in all its full-fledged beauty. Its color was checked black and white like a loon's back, but its name I know not. My chief interest in it, aside from the interest we feel in any new form of life, arose from the creature's extreme anxiety to reach a perch where it could unfold its wings. A little delay would doubtless have been fatal to it. I wonder how many human geniuses are hatched whose wings are blighted

16

by some accident or untoward circumstance. Or do the wings of genius always unfold, no matter what the environment may be?

One seldom takes a walk without encountering some of this fine print on nature's page. Now it is a little yellowish-white moth that spreads itself upon the middle of a leaf as if to imitate the droppings of birds; or it is the young cicadas working up out of the ground, and in the damp, cool places building little chimneys or tubes above the surface to get more warmth and hasten their development; or it is a wood-newt gorging a tree-cricket, or a small snake gorging the newt, or a bird song with some striking peculiarity — a strange defect, or a rare excellence. Now it is a shrike impaling his victim, or blue jays mocking and teasing a hawk and dropping quickly into the branches to avoid his angry blows, or a robin hustling a cuckoo out of the tree where her nest is, or a vireo driving away a cowbird, or the partridge blustering about your feet till her young are hidden. One October morning I was walking along the road on the edge of the woods, when I came into a gentle shower of butternuts; one of them struck my hat-brim. I paused and looked about me; here one fell, there another, yonder a third. There was no wind blowing, and I wondered what was loosening the butternuts. Turning my attention to the top of the tree, I soon saw the explanation: a red squirrel was at work

17

gathering his harvest. He would seize a nut, give it a twist, when down it would come; then he would dart to another and another. Farther along I found where he had covered the ground with chestnut burs; he could not wait for the frost and the winds; did he know that the burs would dry and open upon the ground, and that the bitter covering of the butternuts would soon fall away from the nut?

There are three things that perhaps happen near me each season that I have never yet seen — the toad casting its skin, the snake swallowing its young, and the larvæ of the moth and butterfly constructing their shrouds. It is a mooted question whether or not the snake does swallow its young, but if there is no other good reason for it, may they not retreat into their mother's stomach to feed? How else are they to be nourished? That the moth larva can weave its own cocoon and attach it to a twig seems more incredible. Yesterday, in my walk, I found a firm, silver-gray cocoon, about two inches long and shaped like an Egyptian mummy (probably *Promethea*), suspended from a branch of a bush by a narrow, stout ribbon twice as long as itself. The fastening was woven around the limb, upon which it turned as if it grew there. I would have given something to have seen the creature perform this feat, and then incase itself so snugly in the silken shroud at the end of this tether. By swinging free, its firm, compact case was in no danger from

THE ART OF SEEING THINGS

woodpeckers, as it might have been if resting
directly upon a branch or tree-trunk. Near by was
the cocoon of another species (*Cecropia*) that was
fastened directly to the limb; but this was vague,
loose, and much more involved and net-like. I
have seen the downy woodpecker assaulting one of
these cocoons, but its yielding surface and webby
interior seemed to puzzle and baffle him.

I am interested even in the way each climbing
plant or vine goes up the pole, whether from right
to left, or from left to right, — that is, with the
hands of a clock or against them, — whether it is
under the law of the great cyclonic storms of the
northern hemisphere, which all move against the
hands of a clock, or in the contrary direction, like
the cyclones in the southern hemisphere. I take
pleasure in noting every little dancing whirlwind
of a summer day that catches up the dust or the
leaves before me, and every little funnel-shaped
whirlpool in the swollen stream or river, whether
or not they spin from right to left or the reverse.
If I were in the southern hemisphere, I am sure
I should note whether these things were under the
law of its cyclones in this respect or under the
law of ours. As a rule, our twining plants and
toy whirlwinds copy our revolving storms and go
against the hands of the clock. But there are exceptions. While the bean, the bittersweet, the morn-
ing-glory, and others go up from left to right, the

hop, the wild buckwheat, and some others go up from right to left. Most of our forest trees show a tendency to wind one way or the other, the hard woods going in one direction, and the hemlocks and pines and cedars and butternuts and chestnuts in another. In different localities, or on different geological formations, I find these directions reversed. I recall one instance in the case of a hemlock six or seven inches in diameter, where this tendency to twist had come out of the grain, as it were, and shaped the outward form of the tree, causing it to make, in an ascent of about thirty feet, one complete revolution about a larger tree close to which it grew. On a smaller scale I have seen the same thing in a pine.

Persons lost in the woods or on the plains, or traveling at night, tend, I believe, toward the left. The movements of men and women, it is said, differ in this respect, one sex turning to the right and the other to the left.

I had lived in the world more than fifty years before I noticed a peculiarity about the rays of light one often sees diverging from an opening, or a series of openings, in the clouds, namely, that they are like spokes in a wheel, the hub, or centre, of which appears to be just there in the vapory masses, instead of being, as is really the case, nearly ninety-three millions of miles beyond. The beams of light that come through cracks or chinks in a wall do not converge in this way, but to the eye run parallel to one another. There is another fact: this fan-shaped display of converging rays is always immediately in front of the observer; that is, exactly between him and the sun, so that the central spoke or shaft in his front is always perpendicular. You cannot see this fan to the right or left of the sun, but only between you and it. Hence, as in the case of the rainbow, no two persons see exactly the same rays.

The eye sees what it has the means of seeing, and its means of seeing are in proportion to the love and desire behind it. The eye is informed and sharpened by the thought. My boy sees ducks on the river where and when I cannot, because at certain seasons he thinks ducks and dreams ducks. One season my neighbor asked me if the bees had injured my grapes. I said, "No; the bees never injure my grapes."

"They do mine," he replied; "they puncture the skin for the juice, and at times the clusters are covered with them."

"No," I said, "it is not the bees that puncture the skin; it is the birds."

"What birds?"

"The orioles."

"But I have n't seen any orioles," he rejoined.

"We have," I continued, "because at this season we think orioles; we have learned by experience how destructive these birds are in the vineyard, and we are on the lookout for them; our eyes and ears are ready for them."

If we think birds, we shall see birds wherever we go; if we think arrowheads, as Thoreau did, we shall pick up arrowheads in every field. Some people have an eye for four-leaved clovers; they see them as they walk hastily over the turf, for they already have them in their eyes. I once took a walk with the late Professor Eaton of Yale. He was just then specially interested in the mosses, and he found them, all kinds, everywhere. I can see him yet, every few minutes upon his knees, adjusting his eye-glasses before some rare specimen. The beauty he found in them, and pointed out to me, kindled my enthusiasm also. I once spent a summer day at the mountain home of a well-known literary woman and editor. She lamented the absence of birds about her house. I named a half-dozen or more I had heard or seen in her trees within an hour — the indigo-bird, the purple finch, the yellowbird, the veery thrush, the red-eyed vireo, the song sparrow.

"Do you mean to say you have seen or heard all these birds while sitting here on my porch?" she inquired.

"I really have," I said.

"I do not see them or hear them," she replied, "and yet I want to very much."

"No," said I; "you only *want to want* to see and hear them."

You must have the bird in your heart before you can find it in the bush.

I was sitting in front of a farmhouse one day in company with the local Nimrod. In a maple tree in front of us I saw the great crested flycatcher. I called the hunter's attention to it, and asked him if he had ever seen that bird before. No, he had not; it was a new bird to him. But he probably had seen it scores of times, — seen it without regarding it. It was not the game he was in quest of, and his eye heeded it not.

Human and artificial sounds and objects thrust themselves upon us; they are within our sphere, so to speak: but the life of nature we must meet halfway; it is shy, withdrawn, and blends itself with a vast neutral background. We must be initiated; it is an order the secrets of which are well guarded.

II

THE COMING OF SUMMER

WHO shall say when one season ends and another begins? Only the almanac-makers can fix these dates. It is like saying when babyhood ends and childhood begins, or when childhood ends and youth begins. To me spring begins when the catkins on the alders and the pussy-willows begin to swell; when the ice breaks up on the river and the first sea-gulls come prospecting northward. Whatever the date — the first or the middle or the last of March — when these signs appear, then I know spring is at hand. Her first birds — the bluebird, the song sparrow, the robin, the red-shouldered starling — are here or soon will be. The crows have a more confident caw, the sap begins to start in the sugar maple, the tiny boom of the first bee is heard, the downy woodpecker begins his resonant *tat*, *tat*, *tat*, on the dry limbs, and the cattle in the barnyard low long and loud with wistful looks toward the fields.

The first hint of summer comes when the trees are fully fledged and the nymph Shadow is born. See her cool circles again beneath the trees in the field, or her deeper and cooler retreats in the woods. On the slopes, on the opposite side of the river, there have been for months under the morning and noon sun only slight shadow tracings, a fretwork of shadow lines; but some morning in May I look across and see solid masses of shade falling from the trees athwart the sloping turf. How the eye revels in them! The trees are again clothed and in their right minds; myriad leaves rustle in promise of the coming festival. Now the trees are sentient beings; they have thoughts and fancies; they stir with emotion; they converse together; they whisper or dream in the twilight; they struggle and wrestle with the storm.

"Caught and cuff'd by the gale,"

Tennyson says.

Summer always comes in the person of June, with a bunch of daisies on her breast and clover blossoms in her hands. A new chapter in the season is opened when these flowers appear. One says to himself, "Well, I have lived to see the daisies again and to smell the red clover." One plucks the first blossoms tenderly and caressingly. What memories are stirred in the mind by the fragrance of the one and the youthful face of the other! There is nothing else like that smell of the clover: it is the maidenly breath of summer; it suggests all fresh, buxom, rural things. A field of ruddy, blooming clover,

26

dashed or sprinkled here and there with the snow-white of the daisies; its breath drifts into the road when you are passing; you hear the boom of bees, the voice of bobolinks, the twitter of swallows, the whistle of woodchucks; you smell wild strawberries; you see the cattle upon the hills; you see your youth, the youth of a happy farm-boy, rise before you. In Kentucky I once saw two fields, of one hundred acres each, all ruddy with blooming clover — perfume for a whole county.

The blooming orchards are the glory of May, the blooming clover-fields the distinction of June. Other characteristic June perfumes come from the honey-locusts and the blooming grapevines. At times and in certain localities the air at night and morning is heavy with the breath of the former, and along the lanes and roadsides we inhale the delicate fragrance of the wild grape. The early grasses, too, with their frostlike bloom, contribute something very welcome to the breath of June.

Nearly every season I note what I call the bridal day of summer — a white, lucid, shining day, with a delicate veil of mist softening all outlines. How the river dances and sparkles; how the new leaves of all the trees shine under the sun; the air has a soft lustre; there is a haze, it is not blue, but a kind of shining, diffused nimbus. No clouds, the sky a bluish white, very soft and delicate. It is the nuptial day of the season; the sun fairly takes the earth to be his own, for better or for worse, on such a day, and what marriages there are going on all about us: the marriages of the flowers, of the bees, of the birds. Everything suggests life, love, fruition. These bridal days are often repeated; the serenity and equipoise of the elements combine. They were such days as these that the poet Lowell had in mind when he exclaimed, "What is so rare as a day in June?" Here is the record of such a day, June 1, 1883: "Day perfect in temper, in mood, in everything. Foliage all out except on button-balls and celtis, and putting on its dark green summer color, solid shadows under the trees, and stretching down the slopes. A few indolent summer clouds here and there. A day of gently rustling and curtsying leaves, when the breeze almost seems to blow upward. The fields of full-grown, nodding rye slowly stir and sway like vast assemblages of people. How the chimney swallows chipper as they sweep past! The vireo's cheerful warble echoes in the leafy maples; the branches of the Norway spruce and the hemlocks have gotten themselves new light green tips; the dandelion's spheres of ethereal down rise above the grass: and now and then one of them suddenly goes down: the little chippy, or social sparrow, has thrown itself upon the frail stalk and brought it to the ground, to feed upon its seeds; here it gets the first fruits of the season. The first red and white clover heads have just opened, the

yellow rock-rose and the sweet viburnum are in
bloom; the bird chorus is still full and animated;
the keys of the red maple strew the ground, and the
cotton of the early everlasting drifts upon the air."
For several days there was but little change. " Getting toward the high tide of summer. The air well
warmed up, Nature in her jocund mood, still, all
leaf and sap. The days are idyllic. I lie on my
back on the grass in the shade of the house, and
look up to the soft, slowly moving clouds, and to
the chimney swallows disporting themselves up
there in the breezy depths. No hardening in vege-
tation yet. The moist, hot, fragrant breath of the
fields — mingled odor of blossoming grasses, clover,
daisies, rye — the locust blossoms, dropping. What
a humming about the hives; what freshness in the
shade of every tree; what contentment in the flocks
and herds! The springs are yet full and cold; the
shaded watercourses and pond margins begin to
draw one." Go to the top of the hill on such a
morning, say by nine o'clock, and see how unspeak-
ably fresh and full the world looks. The morning
shadows yet linger everywhere, even in the sunshine; a kind of blue coolness and freshness, the
vapor of dew tinting the air.

Heat and moisture, the father and mother of all
that lives, when June has plenty of these, the increase is sure.

Early in June the rye and wheat heads begin to

nod; the motionless stalks have a reflective, meditative air. A little while ago, when their heads were empty or filled only with chaff and sap, how straight up they held them! Now that the grain is forming, they have a sober, thoughtful look. It is one of the most pleasing spectacles of June, a field of rye gently shaken by the wind. How the breezes are defined upon its surface — a surface as sensitive as that of water; how they trip along, little breezes and big breezes together! Just as this glaucous green surface of the rye-field bends beneath the light tread of the winds, so, we are told, the crust of the earth itself bends beneath the giant strides of the great atmospheric waves.

There is one bird I seldom hear till June, and that is the cuckoo. Sometimes the last days of May bring him, but oftener it is June before I hear his note. The cuckoo is the true recluse among our birds. I doubt if there is any joy in his soul. "Rain-crow," he is called in some parts of the country. His call is supposed to bode rain. Why do other birds, the robin for instance, often make war upon the cuckoo, chasing it from the vicinity of their nests? There seems to be something about the cuckoo that makes its position among the birds rather anomalous. Is it at times a parasitical bird, dropping its eggs into other birds' nests? Or is there some suggestion of the hawk about our species as well as about the European? I do not know. I only know that it seems to be regarded with a suspicious eye by other birds, and that it wanders about at night in a way that no respectable bird should. The birds that come in March, as the bluebird, the robin, the song sparrow, the starling, build in April; the April birds, such as the brown thrasher, the barn swallow, the chewink, the water-thrush, the oven-bird, the chippy, the high-hole, the meadowlark, build in May, while the May birds, the kingbird, the wood thrush, the oriole, the orchard starling, and the warblers, build in June. The April nests are exposed to the most dangers: the storms, the crows, the squirrels, are all liable to cut them off. The midsummer nests, like that of the goldfinch and the waxwing, or cedar-bird, are the safest of all.

In March the door of the seasons first stands ajar a little; in April it is opened much wider; in May the windows go up also; and in June the walls are fairly taken down and the genial currents have free play everywhere. The event of March in the country is the first good sap day, when the maples thrill with the kindling warmth; the event of April is the new furrow and the first seeding; — how ruddy and warm the soil looks just opened to the sun! — the event of May is the week of orchard bloom; with what sweet, pensive gladness one walks beneath the pink-white masses, while long, long thoughts descend upon him! See the impetuous orioles chase one another amid the branches, shaking down the fragrant snow. Here the rose-breasted grosbeak is in the blooming cherry tree, snipping off the blossoms with that heavy beak of his — a spot of crimson and black half hidden in masses of white petals. This orchard bloom travels like a wave. In March it is in the Carolinas; by the middle of April its crest has reached the Potomac; a week or ten days later it is in New Jersey; then in May it sweeps through New York and New England; and early in June it is breaking upon the orchards in Canada. Finally, the event of June is the fields ruddy with clover and milk-white with daisies.

III

A BREATH OF APRIL

I

IT would not be easy to say which is our finest or most beautiful wild flower, but certainly the most poetic and the best beloved is the arbutus. So early, so lowly, so secretive there in the moss and dry leaves, so fragrant, tinged with the hues of youth and health, so hardy and homelike, it touches the heart as no other does.

April's flower offers the first honey to the bee and the first fragrance to the breeze. Modest, exquisite, loving the evergreens, loving the rocks, untamable, it is the very spirit and breath of the woods. Trailing, creeping over the ground, hiding its beauty under withered leaves, stiff and hard in foliage, but in flower like the cheek of a maiden.

One may brush away the April snow and find this finer snow beneath it. Oh, the arbutus days, what memories and longings they awaken! In this latitude they can hardly be looked for before April, and some seasons not till the latter days of the month. The first real warmth, the first tender skies, the first fragrant showers — the woods are flooded with sunlight, and the dry leaves and the leaf-mould emit a pleasant odor. One kneels down or lies down beside a patch of the trailing vine, he brushes away the leaves, he lifts up the blossoming sprays and examines and admires them at leisure; some are white, some are white and pink, a few are deep pink. It is enough to bask there in the sunlight on the ground beside them, drinking in their odor, feasting the eye on their tints and forms, hearing the April breezes sigh and murmur in the pines or hemlocks near you, living in a present fragrant with the memory of other days. Lying there, half dreaming, half observing, if you are not in communion with the very soul of spring, then there is a want of soul in you. You may hear the first swallow twittering from the sky above you, or the first mellow drum of the grouse come up from the woods below or from the ridge opposite. The bee is abroad in the air, finding her first honey in the flower by your side and her first pollen in the pussy-willows by the watercourses below you. The tender, plaintive love-note of the chickadee is heard here and there in the woods. He utters it while busy on the catkins of the poplars, from which he seems to be extracting some kind of food. Hawks are screaming high in the air above the woods; the plow is just tasting the first earth in the rye or corn stubble (and it tastes good). The earth looks good, it smells good, it is good. By the creek in the woods you hear the

34

first water-thrush — a short, bright, ringing, hurried song. If you approach, the bird flies swiftly up or down the creek, uttering an emphatic " chip, chip."

In wild, delicate beauty we have flowers that far surpass the arbutus: the columbine, for instance, jetting out of a seam in a gray ledge of rock, its many crimson and flame-colored flowers shaking in the breeze; but it is mostly for the eye. The spring-beauty, the painted trillium, the fringed polygala, the showy lady's-slipper, are all more striking to look upon, but they do not quite touch the heart; they lack the soul that perfume suggests. Their charms do not abide with you as do those of the arbutus.

II

These still, hazy, brooding mid-April mornings, when the farmer first starts afield with his plow, when his boys gather the buckets in the sugar-bush, when the high-hole calls long and loud through the hazy distance, when the meadowlark sends up her clear, silvery shaft of sound from the meadow, when the bush sparrow trills in the orchard, when the soft maples look red against the wood, or their fallen bloom flecks the drying mud in the road, — such mornings are about the most exciting and sug-gestive of the whole year. How good the fields look, how good the freshly turned earth looks! — one could almost eat it as does the horse; — the stable manure just being drawn out and scattered looks good and smells good; every farmer's house and barn looks inviting; the children on the way to school with their dinner-pails in their hands — how they open a door into the past for you! Sometimes they have sprays of arbutus in their button-holes, or bunches of hepatica. The partridge is drumming in the woods, and the woodpeckers are drumming on dry limbs.

The day is veiled, but we catch such glimpses through the veil. The bees are getting pollen from the pussy-willows and soft maples, and the first honey from the arbutus.

It is at this time that the fruit and seed catalogues are interesting reading, and that the cuts of farm implements have a new fascination. The soil calls to one. All over the country, people are responding to the call, and are buying farms and moving upon them. My father and mother moved upon their farm in the spring of 1828; I moved here upon mine in March, 1874.

I see the farmers, now going along their stone fences and replacing the stones that the frost or the sheep and cattle have thrown off, and here and there laying up a bit of wall that has tumbled down.

There is rare music now in the unmusical call of the phœbe-bird — it is so suggestive.

The drying road appeals to one as it never does at any other season. When I was a farm-boy, it was about this time that I used to get out of my boots for half an hour and let my bare feet feel the ground beneath them once more. There was a smooth, dry, level place in the road near home, and along this I used to run, and exult in that sense of lightfootedness which is so keen at such times. What a feeling of freedom, of emancipation, and of joy in the returning spring I used to experience in those warm April twilights!

I think every man whose youth was spent on the farm, whatever his life since, must have moments at this season when he longs to go back to the soil. How its sounds, its odors, its occupations, its associations, come back to him! Would he not like to return again to help rake up the litter of straw and stalks about the barn, or about the stack on the hill where the grass is starting? Would he not like to help pick the stone from the meadow, or mend the brush fence on the mountain where the sheep roam, or hunt up old Brindle's calf in the woods, or gather oven-wood for his mother to start again the big brick oven with its dozen loaves of rye bread, or see the plow crowding the lingering snow-banks on the side-hill, or help his father break and swingle and hatchel the flax in the barnyard?

When I see a farm advertised for rent or for sale in the spring, I want to go at once and look it over. All the particulars interest me — so many acres of meadow-land, so many of woodland, so many of pasture — the garden, the orchard, the outbuildings, the springs, the creek — I see them all, and am already half in possession.

Even Thoreau felt this attraction, and recorded in his Journal: "I know of no more pleasing employment than to ride about the country with a companion very early in the spring, looking at farms with a view to purchasing, if not paying for them."

Blessed is the man who loves the soil!

III

One mid-April morning two pairs of bluebirds were in very active and at times violent courtship about my grounds. I could not quite understand the meaning of all the fuss and flutter. Both birds of each pair were very demonstrative, but the female in each case the more so. She followed the male everywhere, lifting and twinkling her wings, and apparently seeking to win him by both word and gesture. If she was not telling him by that cheery, animated, confiding, softly-endearing speech of hers, which she poured out incessantly, how much she loved him, what was she saying? She was constantly filled with a desire to perch upon the precise spot where he was sitting, and if he had not moved away, I think she would have alighted upon his back. Now and then, when she flitted away from him, he followed her with like gestures and tones and demonstrations of affection, but never with quite the same ardor. The two pairs kept near each other about the house, the bird-boxes, the trees, the posts and vines in the vineyard, filling the ear with their soft, insistent warbles, and the eye with their twinkling azure wings.

Was it this constant presence of rivals on both sides that so stimulated them and kept them up to such a pitch of courtship? Finally, after I had watched them over an hour, the birds began to come into collision. As they met in the vineyard, the two males clinched and fell to the ground, lying there for a moment with wings sprawled out, like birds brought down by a gun. Then they separated, and each returned to his mate, warbling and twinkling his wings. Very soon the females clinched and fell to the ground and fought savagely, rolling over and over each other, clawing and tweaking and locking beaks and hanging on like bull terriers. They did this repeatedly; once one of the males dashed in and separated them, by giving one of the females a sharp tweak and blow. Then the males were at it again, their blue plumage mixing with the green grass and ruffled by the ruddy soil. What a soft, feathery, ineffectual battle it seemed in both cases; no sound, no blood, no flying feathers, just a sudden mixing up and general disarray of blue wings and tails and ruddy breasts, there on the ground; assault but no visible wounds; thrust of beak and grip of claw, but no feather loosened and but little ruffling; long holding of one down by the other, but no cry of pain or fury. It was the kind of battle that one likes to witness. The birds usually locked beaks, and held their grip half a minute at a time. One of the females would always alight by the struggling males and lift her wings and utter her soft notes, but what she said — whether she was encouraging one of the blue coats or berating the other, or imploring them both to desist, or egging them on — I could not tell. So far as I could understand her speech, it was the same as she had been uttering to her mate all the time.

The language of birds is so limited that one cannot always tell their love-calls from their battle-cries. I recognize three notes in the bluebird — a simple, plaintive call uttered in the air by the migrating birds, both fall and spring, which is like the word "pure," "pure;" then the animated warbling calls and twitterings, during the mating season, which are uttered in a fond, reassuring tone, usually accompanied by that pretty wing gesture; then the call of alarm when some enemy approaches the nest or a hawk appears.

This last note is soft like the others, but the tone is different; it is sorrowful and apprehensive. Most of our song birds have these three notes expressive of love, alarm, and fellowship. The last-named call seems to keep them in touch with one another. I might perhaps add to this list the scream of distress which most birds utter when caught by a cat or a hawk — the voice of uncontrolled terror and pain, which is nearly the same in all species — dissonant and piercing. The other notes and calls are characteristic, but this last is the simple screech of common terrified nature.

When my bluebirds dashed at each other with beak and claw, their preliminary utterances had to my ears anything but a hostile sound. Indeed, for the bluebird to make a harsh, discordant sound seems out of the question. Once, when the two males lay upon the ground with outspread wings and locked beaks, a robin flew down by them and for a moment gazed intently at the blue splash upon the grass, and then went his way.

As the birds drifted about the grounds, first the males, then the females rolling on the grass or in the dust in fierce combat, and between times the members of each pair assuring each other of undying interest and attachment, I followed them, apparently quite unnoticed by them. Sometimes they would lie more than a minute upon the ground, each trying to keep his own or to break the other's hold. They seemed so oblivious of everything about them that I wondered if they might not at such times fall an easy prey to cats and hawks. Let me put their watchfulness to the test, I said. So, as the two males clinched again and fell to the ground, I cautiously approached them, hat in hand. When

41

ten feet away and unregarded, I made a sudden
dash and covered them with my hat. The struggle
continued for a few seconds under there, then all
was still. Sudden darkness had fallen upon the
field of battle. What did they think had happened?
Presently their heads and wings began to brush the
inside of my hat. Then all was still again. Then I
spoke to them, called to them, exulted over them,
but they betrayed no excitement or alarm. Occasionally a head or a body came in gentle contact
with the top or the sides of my hat.

But the two females were evidently agitated by
the sudden disappearance of their contending
lovers, and began uttering their mournful alarm-
note. After a minute or two I lifted one side of my
hat and out darted one of the birds; then I lifted
the hat from the other. One of the females then
rushed, apparently with notes of joy and congratu-
lation, to one of the males, who gave her a spiteful
tweak and blow. Then the other came and he
served her the same. He was evidently a little
bewildered, and not certain what had happened
or who was responsible for it. Did he think the two
females were in some way to blame? But he was
soon reconciled to one of them again, as was the
other male with the other, yet the two couples did
not separate till the males had come in collision
once more. Presently, however, they drifted apart,
and each pair was soon holding an animated con-

versation, punctuated by those pretty wing gestures, about the two bird-boxes.

These scenes of love and rivalry had lasted nearly all the forenoon, and matters between the birds apparently remained as they were before — the members of each pair quite satisfied with each other. One pair occupied one of the bird-boxes in the vineyard and reared two broods there during the season, but the other pair drifted away and took up their abode somewhere else.

If they had come to an understanding, why this continued demonstration and this war between them? The unusual thing was the interest and the activity of the females. They outdid the males in making love and in making war. With most species of our birds, the females are quite indifferent to the blandishments of the males, if they are not actually bored by them. They flee from them, or spitefully resent their advances. In April a female robin may often be seen fighting off three or four of her obstreperous admirers, as if every feminine senti-ment she possessed had been outraged.

But the bluebird is an exception; the female is usually very responsive, but only in the instance above related have I seen her so active in the court-ship.

IV

A WALK IN THE FIELDS

LET us go and walk in the fields. It is the middle of a very early March — a March that has in some way cut out April and got into its place.

I knew an Irish laborer, who during his last illness thought, when spring came, if he could walk in the fields, he would get well. I have observed that farmers, when harassed by trouble, or weighed down by grief, are often wont to go and walk alone in the fields. They find dumb sympathy and companionship there. I knew a farmer who, after the death of his only son, would frequently get up in the middle of the night and go and walk in his fields. It was said that he had been harsh and unjust to his son, and, during the last day the latter had worked and when the fatal illness was coming upon him, the father had severely upbraided him because he left his task and sat for a while under the fence. One can fancy him going to this very spot in his midnight wanderings, and standing in mute agony where the cruel words had been spoken, or throwing himself upon the ground, pleading in vain at the door of the irrevocable past. That door

45

never opens again, plead you there till your heart
breaks.

A farmer's fields become in time almost a part
of himself: his life history is written all over them;
virtue has gone out of himself into them; he has
fertilized them with the sweat of his brow; he knows
the look and the quality of each one. This one he
reclaimed from the wilderness when he came on the
farm as a young man; he sowed rye among the
stumps and scratched it in with a thorn brush; as
the years went by he saw the stumps slowly decay;
he would send his boys to set fire to them in the dry
spring weather; — I was one of those boys, and it
seems as if I could smell the pungent odor of those
burning stumps at this moment: now this field is
one of his smoothest, finest meadows. This one was
once a rough pasture; he pried up or blasted out
the rocks, and with his oxen drew them into a
line along the border of the woods, and with stone
picked or dug from the surface built upon them a
solid four-foot wall; now the mowing-machine runs
evenly where once the cattle grazed with difficulty.

I was a boy when that field was cleaned up. I took
a hand — a boy's hand — in the work. I helped pick
up the loose stone, which we drew upon a stone-boat
shod with green poles. It was back-aching work, and
it soon wore the skin thin on the ends of the fingers.
How the crickets and ants and beetles would rush
about when we uncovered them! They no doubt

looked upon the stone that sheltered them as an old institution that we had no right to remove. No right, my little folk, only the might of the stronger. Sometimes a flat stone would prove the roof of a mouse-nest — a blinking, bead-eyed, meadow-mouse. What consternation would seize him, too, as he would rush off along the little round beaten ways under the dry grass and weeds! Many of the large bowlders were deeply imbedded in the soil, and only stuck their noses or heads, so to speak, up through the turf. These we would first tackle with the big lever, a long, dry, ironwood pole, as heavy as one could handle, shod with a horseshoe. With the end of this thrust under the end or edge of a bowlder, and resting upon a stone for a fulcrum, we would begin the assault. Inch by inch the turf-bound rock would yield. Sometimes the lever would slip its hold, and come down upon our heads if we were not watchful. As the rock yielded, the lever required more bait, as the farmer calls it, — an addition to the fulcrum. After the rock was raised sufficiently, we would prop it up with stones, arrange a skid or skids under it — green beech poles cut in the woods — wrap a chain around it, and hitch the oxen to it, directing them to the right or left to turn the bowlder out of its bed and place it on the surface of the ground. When this was accomplished, then came the dead straight pull to the line of the fence. An old, experienced ox-team know what is before them, or rather behind them; they have felt the bowlder and sized it up. At the word and the crack of the whip they bend their heads and throw their weight upon the yoke. Now the hickory bows settle into their shoulders, they kink their tails and hump their backs, their sharp hoofs cut the turf, and the great inert mass moves. Tearing up the sod, grinding over stones, the shouts of the excited driver urging them on, away they go toward the line. The peculiar and agreeable odor of burnt and ground stone arises from the rear. Only a few yards at a time; how the oxen puff as they halt to take breath and lap their tongues out over their moist muzzles! Then they bend to the work again, the muscular effort reaching their very tails. Thus the work goes on for several days or a week, till the row of bottom rocks is complete. If there are others remaining in the field, then the row is doubled up till the land is cleaned.

What a torn and wounded appearance that section of ground presents, its surface everywhere marked with red stripes or bands, each ending in or starting from a large and deep red cavity in the sward! But soon the plow will come, equalizing and obliterating and writing another history upon the page.

There is something to me peculiarly interesting in stone walls — a kind of rude human expression to them, suggesting the face of the old farmer himself. How they climb the hills and sweep through the valleys. They decay not, yet they grow old and decrepit; little by little they lose their precision and firmness, they stagger, then fall. In a still, early spring morning or April twilight one often hears a rattle of stones in a distant field; some bit of old wall is falling. The lifetime of the best of them is rarely threescore and ten. The other day, along the highway, I saw an old man relaying a dilapidated stone wall. "Fifty-three years ago," he said, "I laid this wall. When it is laid again, I shan't have the job." It is rarely now that one sees a new wall going up. The fences have all been built, and the farmer has only to keep them in repair.

When you build a field or a highway wall, do not make the top of it level across the little hollows; let it bend to the uneven surface, let it look flexible and alive. A foundation wall, with its horizontal lines, looks stiff and formal, but a wall that undulates along like a live thing pleases the eye.

When I was a boy upon the old farm, my father always "laid out" to build forty or fifty rods of new wall, or rebuild as many rods of old wall, each spring. It is true husbandry to fence your field with the stones that incumber it, to utilize obstacles. The walls upon the old farm of which I am thinking have each a history. This one, along the lower side of the road, was built in '46. I remember the man who laid it. I even remember something of the complexion of the May days when the work was going on. It was built from a still older wall, and new material added. It leans and staggers in places now like an old man, but it is still a substantial fence. This one upon the upper side of the road, my father told me he built the year he came upon the farm, which was in '28. He paid twenty cents a rod for having it laid to a man whose grandchildren are now gray-haired men. The wall has a rock foundation, and it still holds its course without much wavering.

The more padding there is in a stone wall, the less enduring it is. Let your stone reach clean through. A smooth face will not save it; a loose and cobbly interior will be its ruin. Let there be a broad foundation, let the parts be well bound together, let the joints be carefully broken, and, above all, let its height not be too great for its width. If it is too high, it will topple over; if its interior is defective, it will spread and collapse. Time searches out its every weakness, and respects only good material and good workmanship.

V

GAY PLUMES AND DULL

I

NOT long since, one of our younger naturalists
sent me a photograph of a fawn in a field of
daisies, and said that he took the picture to show
what he considered the protective value of the spots.
The white spots of the fawn did blend in with the
daisies, and certainly rendered the fawn less conspicuous than it would have been without them,
but I am slow to believe that the fawn has spots that
it may the better hide in a daisy-field, or, in fact,
anywhere else, or that the spots have ever been
sufficiently protective to have materially aided in
the perpetuity of the deer species. What use they
have, if any, I do not know, any more than I know
what use the spots on the leopard or the giraffe
have, or the stripes on the zebra. I can only conjecture concerning their use. The panther does
not have spots, and seems to get along just as well
without them. The young of the moose and the
caribou and the pronghorn are not spotted, and yet
their habitat is much the same as that of the deer.

Why some forest animals are uniformly dark

colored, while others are more or less brilliantly striped or spotted, is a question not easily answered. It is claimed that spotted and striped species are more diurnal in their habits, and frequent bushes and open glades, while the dusky species are more nocturnal, and frequent dense thickets. In a general way this is probably true. A dappled coat is more in keeping with the day than with the night, and with bushes and jungles rather than with plains or dense forests. But whether its protective value, or the protective value of the dusky coat, is the reason for its being, is another question.

This theory of the protective coloration of animals has been one of the generally accepted ideas in all works upon natural history since Darwin's time. It assumes that the color of an animal is as much the result of natural selection as any part of its structure — natural selection picking out and preserving those tints that were the most useful in concealing the animal from its enemies or from its prey. If in this world no animal had ever preyed upon another, it is thought that their colors might have been very different, probably much more bizarre and inharmonious than they are at present.

Now I am not going to run amuck upon this generally accepted theory of modern naturalists, but I do feel disposed to shake it up a little, and to see, if I can, what measure of truth there is in it. That there is a measure of truth in it I am con-

A Fawn

vinced, but that it has been greatly overworked in our time, and that more has been put upon it than it can bear, of this also I am convinced.

I think we are safe in saying that a bird is protectively colored when the color, as it were, strikes in, and the bird itself acts upon the theory that it is in a measure hidden behind its assimilative plumage. This is true of nearly all the grouse tribe. These birds seem instinctively to know the value of their imitative tints, and are tame or wild according as their tints do or do not match the snow on the ground. The snow keeps the secrets of the snow, and the earth keeps the secrets of the earth, but each tells upon the other. Sportsmen tell me that quail will not "lay" when there is snow upon the ground. The snow gives them away; it lights up their covers in the weeds and the bog as with a lamp. At other times the quail will "lay" till the hunter almost steps upon them. His dog sometimes picks them up. What is the meaning of this behavior but that the bird feels hidden in the one case and not in the other? Moreover, the grouse are all toothsome; and this fact of the toothsomeness of some birds and the toughness and unsavoriness of others, such as the woodpecker, the crow tribe, gulls, divers, cormorants, and the like, has undoubtedly played some part in their natural history. But whether they are dull-colored because they are toothsome, or toothsome because they are dull-colored — who shall say? Which was first, the sweetness or the color? The flesh of the quail and the partridge having become very delectable and much sought after by many wild creatures, did Nature make compensation by giving them their assimilative plumage? or were the two facts insep- arable from the first? Yet the flesh of the peacock is said to be as delicate as that of the turkey.

The sweetness of an animal's flesh is doubtless determined by its food. I believe no one eats the Western road-runner, though it is duller of color than the turkey. Its food is mice, snakes, lizards, centipedes, and other vermin.

Thus far I can follow the protective-colorists, but not much farther.

Wallace goes to the extent of believing that even nuts are protectively colored because they are not to be eaten. But without the agency of birds and the small rodents, the wingless nuts, such as chest- nuts, acorns, hickory nuts, and butternuts, could never get widely scattered; so that if they were effectively concealed by their colors, this fact would tend to their extinction.

If the colors of animals were as vital a matter, and the result of the same adaptive and selective process, as their varied structures, which Darwin and Wallace teach, then it would seem to follow that those of the same habits and of the same or similar habitat would be similar or identical in

color, which is not commonly the case. Thus among
the birds, the waders all have long legs and long
necks, but they are not all of the same color. The
divers all have short legs placed in the rear, but
they vary greatly in color-markings. How greatly
the ducks differ in coloration, though essentially
the same in structure! Our tree warblers are of all
hues and combinations of hues, though so alike in
habit and form. The painted bunting in the South-
west is gaudily colored, while its congeners are all
more plainly dressed.

In England the thrush that answers to our robin,
being almost identical in form, manner, and habit,
is black as a coal. The crow tribe are all built upon
the same plan, and yet they show a very great diversity of colors. Why is our jay so showily colored,
and the Canada jay so subdued in tint?

The hummingbirds do not differ much in their
anatomy, but their tints differ as much as do those
of precious stones. The woodpeckers show a variety
of markings that cannot be accounted for upon any
principle of utility or of natural selection. Indeed,
it would seem as if in the colors of birds and mammals Nature gave herself a comparatively free hand,
not being bound by the same rigid necessity as in
their structures. Within certain limits, something
like caprice or accident seems to prevail. The great
law of assimilation, or harmonious blending, of
which I shall presently have more to say, goes on,

but it is checked and thwarted and made sport of by other tendencies.

Then the principle of coloration of the same species does not always hold good in different parts of the earth. Our northern flycatchers are all of dull plumage, but in Mexico we find the vermilion flycatcher, with under parts of bright scarlet, and in Java is a flycatcher like a flame of fire. With us, as soon as a bird touches the ground it takes on some ground colors. All our ground-feeders are more or less ground-tinted. But in the East this is not to the same extent true. Thus our pigeons and doves are blue-gray and buff. In the Molucca Islands there is a blue and purple dove, and one species with coppery green plumage, a snow-white tail, and snow-white pendent feathers on the neck. Our thrushes are ground-feeders and are ground-colored. The ground thrushes of the Malay Archipelago are much more brilliantly marked. One species has the "upper parts soft green, the head jet black, with a stripe of blue and brown over the eye; at the base of the tail and on the shoulders are bands of bright silvery blue, and the under-sides are of delicate buff with a stripe of rich crimson bordered with black on the belly." Another ground thrush is velvety black above, relieved by a breast of pure white, shoulders of azure blue, and belly of vivid crimson — one of the most beautiful birds of the East, Wallace says. The Eastern kingfishers are

also much more brilliant than ours. Our gallina-
ceous birds are all dull neutral-tinted, but look at
this family of birds in the Orient, brilliant beyond
words to paint! In Africa the sand grouse is brilliantly marked. There are also snow-white herons
in Africa, and black and white ibises. On the Aru
Islands in the Malay Archipelago is a flycatcher
that is brilliant black and bright orange.

In our hemisphere the swans are white, the
pigeons are blue, and the parrots are green. In
Australia the swans are black, and there is a black
pigeon and a black parrot. In the desert of Sahara
most of the birds are desert-colored, but there are
some that are blue, and others that are black or
brown and white. It is said that the Arctic fox,
which is snow-white in most other places, remains
blue all winter in Iceland. No doubt there are
reasons for all these variations, but whatever these
reasons are, they do not seem to favor the theory
of protective coloration.

The more local an animal is, the more its color
assimilates with its surroundings; or perhaps I
should say, the more uniform its habitat, the more
assimilative its coloring. The valley quail of California frequents trees and roosts in trees, hence
its coloring is not copied from the ground. It is
darker and bluer than our Bob White.

Nature dislikes incongruities, and permits them
under protest. The fleet rabbit with eyes ever open

is as protectively colored as the toad or the tortoise. The porcupine with his armor of quills is as hidden from the eye as the coon, or the woodchuck, or the prairie-dog. Climbing things are as well hidden as creeping things, the mole in the ground as well as the mouse on the surface, the squirrel that flies as well as the squirrel that runs, creatures of the night as well as creatures of the day, the elephant, the rhinoceros, the hippopotamus, as well as the smaller animals that are preyed upon. If birds are colored to conceal them from hawks, why are the wild boar, the deer, the hare, similarly colored? They are not hiding from hawks; their enemies go by scent. The hippopotamus in the Nile is as protectively colored as the camel on the sands, and yet in neither case can protection be the end sought. In Africa there is a white rhinoceros. Behold our mountain goat nearly as white as snow against the dark background of the rocks and mountain-slopes where he lives, and yet he appears to thrive as well as the protectively colored deer. Does not the lion without stripes fare just as well as the tiger with? Does not our vermilion flycatcher fare just as well as its cousins of duller plumes? Does not the golden pheasant fare as well as the protectively colored grouse? Everywhere the creative energy seems to have its plain, modest moods and its gaudy, bizarre moods, both in the vegetable and the animal worlds. Why are some flowers so gaudy and others

so plain, some so conspicuous and others so hidden, some insects so brilliant and others so dull,
some fruits so highly colored and others so neutral?
This law of endless variation is no doubt at the
bottom of all these things. The bird has varied
in color from its parent, and as the variation has
not told against it, it has gone on and intensified.
So with the flowers. I don't believe cherries are red
or black to attract the birds, or plums blue. Poisonous berries are as brilliant as harmless ones. No
doubt there is a reason for all these high colors,
and for the plain ones, if we could only find it. Of
course, food, environment, climate, have much to
do with it all.

Probably, if we could compare the food which
our grouse eats with that which the brilliant pheasants of the East eat, or the food of our wild turkey
with that of the Central American bird, or of our
pigeons with those of the Malay Archipelago, we
might hit upon some clue to their difference of coloration. The strange and bizarre colors and forms
of the birds of Africa compared with those of North
America or of Europe may be a matter of food. Why
our flicker is brighter colored than our other woodpeckers may be on account of the ants he eats.

Mr. Wallace in one of his essays points out the
effect of locality on color, many species of unrelated
genera both among insects and among birds being
marked similarly, with white or yellow or black,

as if from the effect of some fashion that has spread among them. In the Philippine Islands metallic hues are the fashion; in some other islands very light tints are in vogue; in still other localities unrelated species favor crimson or blue. Mr. Wallace says that among the various butterflies of different countries this preference for certain colors is as marked as it would be if the hares, marmots, and squirrels of Europe were all red with black feet, while the corresponding species of Central Asia were all yellow with black heads, or as it would be if our smaller mammals, the coon, the possum, the squirrels, all copied the black and white of the skunk. The reason for all this is not apparent, though Wallace thinks that some quality of the soil which affects the food may be the cause. It is like the caprice of fashion. In fact, the exaggerated plumes, fantastic colors, and monstrous beaks of many birds in both hemispheres have as little apparent utility, and seem to be quite as much the result of caprice, as are any of the extreme fashions in dress among human beings.

Our red-shouldered starlings flock in the fall, and they are not protectively colored, but the bobolinks, which also flock at the same time, do then assume neutral tints. Why the change in the one case and not in the other, since both species feed in the brown marshes? Most of our own ground birds are more or less ground-colored; but here on the ground, amid

the bushes, with the brown oven-bird and the brown
thrasher, is the chewink with conspicuous markings of white and black and red. Here are some
of the soft gray and brown tinted warblers nesting
on the ground, and here is the more conspicuous
striped black and white creeping warbler nesting
by their side. Behold the rather dull-colored great
crested flycatcher concealing its nest in a hollow
limb, and its congener the brighter-feathered kingbird building its nest openly on the branch above.

Hence, whatever truth there may be in this theory
of protective coloration, one has only to look about
him to discover that it is a matter which Nature
does not have very much at heart. She plays fast
and loose with it on every hand. Now she seems to
set great store by it, the next moment she discards
it entirely.

If dull colors are protective, then bright colors
are non-protective or dangerous, and one wonders
why all birds of gay feather have not been cut off
and the species exterminated: or why, in cases
where the males are bright-colored and the females
of neutral tints, as with our scarlet tanager and
indigo-bird, the females are not greatly in excess of
the males, which does not seem to be the case.

II

We arrive at the idea that neutral tints are protective from the point of view of the human eye.

Now if all animals that prey upon others were guided by the eye alone, there would be much more in the theory than there is. But none of the predaceous four-footed beasts depend entirely upon the eye. The cat tribe does to a certain extent, but these creatures stalk or waylay moving game, and the color does not count. A white hare will evidently fall a prey to a lynx or a cougar in our winter woods as easily as a brown rabbit; and will not a desert-colored animal fall a prey to a lion or a tiger just as readily as it would if it were white or black? Then the most destructive tribes of all, the wolves, the foxes, the minks, the weasels, the skunks, the coons, and the like, depend entirely upon scent. The eye plays a very insignificant part in their hunting, hence again the question of color is eliminated.

Birds of prey depend upon the eye, but they are also protectively colored, and their eyes are so preternaturally sharp that no disguise of assimilative tints is of any avail against them. If both the hunted and its hunter are concealed by their neutral tints, of what advantage is it to either? If the brown bird is hidden from the brown hawk, and *vice versa*, then are they on an equal footing in this respect, and the victory is to the sharpest-eyed. If, as is doubtless the case, the eye of the hawk sharpens as the problem of his existence becomes more difficult, then is the game even, and the quarry

has no advantage — the protective color does not
protect.

Why should the owl, which hunts by night, be
colored like the hawk that hunts by day? If
the owl were red, or blue, or green, or black, or
white, would it not stand just as good a chance of
obtaining a subsistence? Its silent flight, its keen-
ness of vision, and the general obscurity are the
main matters. At night color is almost neutralized.
Would not the lynx and the bobcat fare just as well
if they were of the hue of the sable or the mink?
Are their neutral grays or browns any advantage to
them? The gray fox is more protectively colored
than the red; is he therefore more abundant? Far
from it; just the reverse is true. The same remark
applies to the red and the gray squirrels.

The northern hare, which changes to white in
winter, would seem to have an advantage over the
little gray rabbit, which is as conspicuous upon
the snow as a brown leaf, and yet such does not
seem to be the case. It is true that the rabbit often
passes the day in holes and beneath rocks, and
the hare does not; but it is only at night that the
natural enemies of each — foxes, minks, weasels,
wildcats, owls — are abroad.

It is thought by Wallace and others that the
skunk is strikingly marked as a danger signal, its
contrast of black and white warning all creatures
to pass by on the other side. But the magpie is

marked in much the same way, as is also our bobolink, which, in some localities, is called "the skunk-bird," and neither of these birds has any such reason to advertise itself as has the skunk. Then here is the porcupine, with its panoply of spears, as protectively colored as the coon or the woodchuck, — why does not it have warning colors also? The enemy that attacks it fares much worse than in the case of its black and white neighbor.

The ptarmigan is often cited as a good illustration of the value of protective coloration, — white in winter, particolored in spring, and brown in summer, — always in color blending with its environment. But the Arctic fox would not be baffled by its color; it goes by scent; and the great snowy owl would probably see it in the open at any time of year. On islands in Bering Sea we saw the Arctic snowbird in midsummer, white as a snowflake, and visible afar. Our northern grouse carry their gray and brown tints through our winters, and do not appear to suffer unduly from their telltale plumage. If the cold were as severe as it is farther north, doubtless they, too, would don white coats, for the extreme cold seems to play an important part in this matter, — this and the long Arctic nights. Sir John Ross protected a Hudson's Bay lemming from the low temperature by keeping it in his cabin, and the animal retained its summer coat; but when he exposed it to a temperature of thirty degrees below zero, it began to change to white in a single night, and at the end of a week was almost entirely so. It is said that in Siberia domestic cattle and horses become lighter-colored in the winter, and Darwin says he has known brown ponies in England to become white during the same season.

Only one of our weasels, the ermine, becomes white in winter; the others keep their brown coats through the year. Is this adaptive color any advantage to the ermine? and are the other weasels handicapped by their brown tints?

The marten, the sable, and the fisher do not turn white in the cold season, nor the musk ox, nor the reindeer. The latter animals are gregarious, and the social spirit seems to oppose local color.

Apart from the intense cold, the long Arctic nights no doubt have much to do with the white of Arctic animals. "Absence of light leads to diminution or even total abolition of pigmentation, while its presence leads to an increase in some degree proportionate to the intensity of the light."[1]

When the variable northern hare is removed to a milder climate, in the course of a few years it ceases to turn white in winter.

The more local an animal is, the more does it incline to take on the colors of its surroundings, as may be seen in the case of the toads, the frogs, the snakes, and many insects. It seems reasonable

[1] Vernon on *Variation in Animals and Plants.*

that the influence of the environment should be more potent in such cases. The grasshoppers in the fields are of all shades of green and brown and gray, but is it probable that these tints ever hide them from their natural enemies — the sharp-eyed birds and fowls? A grasshopper gives itself away when it hops, and it always hops. On the sea-coast I noticed that the grasshoppers were gray like the sands. What fed upon them, if anything, I could not find out, but their incessant hopping showed how little they sought concealment. The nocturnal enemies of grasshoppers, such as coons and skunks, are probably not baffled at all by their assimilative colors.

Our wood-frog (*Rana sylvatica*) is found through-out the summer on the dry leaves in the woods, and it is red like them. When it buries itself in the leaf mould in the fall for its winter sleep, it turns dark like the color of the element in which it is buried. Can this last change be for protection also? No enemy sees it or disturbs it in that position, and yet it is as "protectively" colored as in summer. This is the stamp of the environment again.

The toad is of the color of the ground where he fumbles along in the twilight or squats by day, and yet, I fancy, his enemy the snake finds him out without difficulty. He is of the color of the earth because he is of the earth earthy, and the bullfrog is of the color of his element, — but there are the little green frog, and the leopard frog, and the pickerel frog, all quite showily marked. So there we are, trying to tabulate Nature when she will not be tabulated! Whether it be the phrase "protective coloration," or the imprint of the environment, with which we seek to capture her, she will not always be captured. In the tropics there are gaudily colored tree-frogs, — blue, yellow, striped, — frogs with red bodies and blue legs, and these showy creatures are never preyed upon, they are uneatable. But the old question comes up again — are the colors to advertise their uneatableness, or are they the necessary outcome, and would they be the same in a world where no living thing was preyed upon by another? The acids or juices that make their flesh unpalatable may be the same that produce the bright colors. To confound the cause with the effect is a common error. I doubt if the high color of some poisonous mushrooms is a warning color, or has any reference to outward conditions. The poison and the color are probably inseparable.

The muskrat's color blends him with his surroundings, and yet his enemies, the mink, the fox, the weasel, trail him just the same; his color does not avail. The same may be said of the woodchuck. What color could he be but earth color? and yet the wolf and the fox easily smell him out. If he were snow-white or jet-black (as he sometimes is), he would be in no greater danger.

I think it highly probable that our bluebird is a descendant of a thrush. The speckled breast of the young bird indicates this, as does a thrush-like note which one may occasionally hear from it. The bird departed from the protective livery of the thrush and came down its long line of descent in a showy coat of blue, and yet got on just as well as its ancestors. Gay plumes were certainly no handicap in this case. Are they in any case? I seriously doubt it. In fact, I am inclined to think that if the birds and the mammals of the earth had been of all the colors of the rainbow, they would be just about as numerous.

The fact that this assimilative coloring disappears in the case of animals under domestication, — that the neutral grays and browns are followed by white and black and particolored animals, — what does that prove? It proves only that the order of Nature has been interfered with, and that as wild instinct becomes demoralized under domestication, so does the wild coloration of animals. The conditions are changed, numberless new influences are brought to bear, the food is changed and is of greater variety, climatic influences are interfered with, multitudes of new and strange impressions are made upon each individual animal, and Nature abandons her uniformity of coloration and becomes reckless, so to speak, not because the pressure of danger is removed, but because the danger is of a

GAY PLUMES AND DULL

new and incalculable kind — the danger from man and artificial conditions. Man demoralizes Nature whenever he touches her, in savage tribes and in animal life, as well as in the fields and woods. He makes sharp contrasts wherever he goes, in forms, in colors, in sounds, in odors, and it is not to be wondered at that animals brought under his influence come in time to show, more or less, these contrasts. The tendency to variation is stimulated; form as well as color is rapidly modified; the old order is broken up, and the animal comes to partake more or less of the bizarre condition that surrounds it. Nature when left to herself is harmonious; man makes discords, or harmony of another order. The instincts of wild animals are much more keen and invariable than are those of animals in domestication, the conditions of their lives being far more rigid and exacting. Remove the eggs from a wild bird's nest and she instantly deserts it; but a domestic fowl will incubate an empty nest for days. For the same reason the colors of animals in domestication are less constant than in the wild state; they break up and become much more bizarre and capricious.

Cultivated plants depart more from a fixed type than do plants of the fields and the woods. See what *outré* forms and colors the cultivated flowers display!

The pressure of fear is of course much greater

upon the wild creatures than upon the tame, but that the removal or the modification of this should cause them to lose their neutral tints is not credible. The domestic pigeons and the barnyard fowls are almost as much exposed to their arch enemy, the hawk, as is the wild pigeon or the jungle fowl, if not more, since the wild birds are free to rush to the cover of the trees and woods. And how ceaseless their vigilance! what keen eyes they have for hawks, whether they circle in the air or walk about in the near fields! In fact, the instinct of fear of some enemy in the air above has apparently not been diminished in the barnyard fowls by countless generations of domestication. Let a boy shy a rusty pie-tin or his old straw hat across the henyard, and behold what a screaming and a rushing to cover there is! This ever watchful fear on the part of the domestic fowls ought to have had some effect in preserving their neutral tints, but it has not. A stronger influence has come from man's disrupture of natural relations.

Why are ducks more variously and more brilliantly colored than geese? I think it would be hard to name the reason. A duck seems of a more intense nature than a goose, more active, more venturesome; it takes to the bypaths, as it were, while the goose keeps to a few great open highways; its range is wider, its food supply is probably more various, and hence it has greater adaptiveness and variabil-

ity. The swan is still more restricted in its range
and numbers than the goose, and, in our hemisphere, is snow-white. The factor of protective coloration, so pronounced in the case of the goose, is
quite ignored in the swan. Neither the goose nor
the swan, so far as I know, has any winged enemies,
but their eggs and young are doubtless in danger
at times from foxes and wolves and water animals.
The duck must have more enemies, because it is
smaller, and is found in more diverse and sundry
places. Upon the principle that like begets like,
that variety breeds variety, one would expect the
ducks to be more brightly and variously colored
than their larger congeners, the geese and the
swans.

The favorite notion of some writers on natural
history, that it is a protective device when animals
are rendered less conspicuous by being light beneath and dark above, seems to me a hasty conclusion. This gradation in shading is an inevitable
result of certain fixed principles. It applies to inanimate objects also. The apples on the tree and
the melons in the garden are protectively shaded
in the same way; they are all lighter beneath
and deeper-colored above. The mushrooms on
the stumps and trees are brown above and white
beneath. Where the light is feeblest the color is
lightest, and *vice versa*. The under side of a bird's
wing is, as a rule, lighter than the top side. The

stronger the light, the more the pigments are developed. All fish that I am acquainted with are light beneath and dark above. If this condition helps to conceal them from their enemies, it is merely incidental, and not the result of laws working to that end.

III

"The danger of the mother bird during incubation" is a phrase often used by Darwin and by more recent writers. This danger is the chief reason assigned for the more obscure coloring of the female among so many species. Now it would seem that the dangers of the mother bird during incubation ought to be far less than those of her more brilliantly colored mate, flitting from tree to tree and advertising his whereabouts by his calls and song, or absorbed in procuring his food; or than those of other females, flying about exposed to the eye of every passing hawk. The life of most wild creatures is like that of a people engaged in war: enemies lurk on every hand, and the danger to the sitting bird may be compared in degree to that of the wife rocking the cradle by her fireside; while her roving mate must face perils equal to those of a soldier on a campaign. The mother bird is generally well hidden, and has nothing to do but to use her eyes and ears, and she usually does this to good purpose. Indeed, I believe the sitting bird is rarely destroyed. I have never known it to happen, though this fact does not prove very much. The peril is to the eggs or to the unfledged young; these cannot run or fly away. Eliminate this danger — this and the danger from storms and cold — and the numbers of our birds would probably double in a single year. Hence the care the birds take to conceal their nests, not for the mother bird's sake, but for the sake of the treasures which she cannot defend. In some cases she appears to offer herself an easy victim in order to lure the intruder away. She would have him see only herself when she flutters, apparently disabled, over the ground. The game of concealment has failed; now she will try what feigning can do.

All the species of our birds in which the male is more brilliantly colored than the female, such as the scarlet tanager, the indigo-bird, the rose-breasted grosbeak, the goldfinch, the summer tanager, the Virginia cardinal, the blue grosbeak, build in trees or low bushes, and it seems to me that the dull tints of the female would play but little part in concealing the nest. The enemies of these birds — as of most of our birds — are crows, squirrels, black snakes, jays, weasels, owls, and hawks, and have been for untold generations. Now the obscure coloring of the female would play no part in protecting her against any of these creatures. What would attract their attention would be the nest itself. The crows, the jays, the weasels, the squirrels, explore the trees looking for eggs and young birds, as doubtless the owls do by night. The mother bird flies at their approach, and leaves her eggs or young to be devoured. The sitting bird usually is not visible to an enemy passing in the air above, as she is hidden by the leaves. In the care of the young the male is as active and as much exposed to danger as is the female, and in the case of the scarlet tanager the male seems the bolder and the more active of the two; yet the female, because of her obscure coloring, could afford to run many more chances than he.

With the ground-builders the case is not much different. These birds are preyed upon by prowlers, — skunks, weasels, rats, snakes, crows, minks, foxes, and cats, — enemies that hunt at close range by night and by day, and that search the ground by sight and by smell. It is not the parent bird, but the eggs and the young, that they capture. Indeed, I cannot see that the color of the sitting bird enters into the problem at all. Red or white or blue would not endanger the nest any more than would the neutral grays and browns. The bobolink builds in meadows where the grass alone conceals it. That the back of the sitting bird harmonizes perfectly with the meadow bottom might make a difference to the egg-collector, or to an eye a few feet above, but not to the mink, or the skunk, or the snake, or the fox, that came nosing about the very spot.

Last summer I saw where a woodcock had made

her nest in a dry, grassy field many yards from a swamp in the woods, which was her natural habitat. The instinct of the bird seemed to tell her that she would be less exposed to her prowling enemies in the dry, open field than in the thick, swampy woods, and her instinct was, no doubt, a safe guide. Her imitative color would avail her but little in either place. The same may be said of the quail and of the grouse. Their neutral tints may protect them from the human eye, but not from their natural enemies. Could the coon, or the mink, or the fox, or the skunk be baffled by them? Is the setter or pointer baffled? Both the quail and the partridge, in settled countries, are very likely to nest along roads and paths, away from thick jungles and tangles that would afford cover to their enemies. It is their eggs and their newly hatched young that they are solicitous about. Their wings afford security to themselves. True, the sitting bird usually allows the passer-by to approach her very closely, but I have reason to believe that she is much sooner alarmed by an animal that approaches stealthily, nosing about, making very little noise, than by the passing of a person or of the large grazing animals. Her old traditional enemies are stealthy and subtle, and her instinct keeps her on her guard against them. A person walking boldly along, occupied about his own business, can pass within a few feet of a partridge on his drumming log. But let a man try to creep up on the drumming partridge, and the bird will instantly show how wary and suspicious he is.

The female cowbird is much duller in color than the male, and yet she is a parasitical bird, and does no incubating at all. With the rose-breasted grosbeak, the male seems to do his share of the incubating, and has been heard to sing upon the nest.

A fact that seems to tell against the notions I have been advancing, and that gives support to the theory of the protective value of dull colors, is the fact that with those species of birds in which both sexes are brightly colored, the nest is usually placed in a hole, or is domed, thus concealing the sitting bird. This is true of a large number of species, as the bluebird, the woodpeckers, the chickadee, the nuthatch, the kingfisher, and, in the tropics, the various species of parrots and parrakeets and many others, all birds of brilliant plumage, the sexes being in each case indistinguishable. But there are such marked exceptions to this rule that, it seems to me, its force is greatly weakened. Our blue jay is a highly colored bird, and yet it builds an open nest. The crow builds an open nest. The passenger pigeon was a bird of rather showy colors, and the male did his share of the incubating, still the nest was built openly. The shrike is a conspicuously marked bird, and it builds an open nest. Mr. Wallace names four other brilliant Old-World birds that build open nests. Then there are several

species of birds, in which the female is obscurely
marked, that build in holes and cavities, such as our
wrens, the great crested flycatcher, the European
starling, the English sparrow, the bush-tits of California, and the wood duck. The female oriole is
much duller-colored than her mate, yet she builds
a pocket nest. Of course these last cases do not
prove that there is not greater safety in a hidden
nest, they only show that the color of the mother
bird is not the main factor in the problem. But
that a bird in a hole is safer than a bird in an open
nest may well be doubted. The eggs are probably
more secure from the thievish crow and the blue
jay, but not from rats and squirrels and weasels.
I know that the nests of the bluebird and the chickadee are often broken up by some small enemy.

We fancy that the birds are guided by their
instinct for protective colors in the materials they
choose for their nests. Most birds certainly aim
to conceal their nests — the solitary builders, but
not those that nest in communities, like the cliff
swallows and rooks and flamingoes — and the
materials they use favor this concealment. But
what other materials could they use? They choose
the material everywhere near at hand, — moss,
leaves, dry grass, twigs, mud, and the like. The
ground-builders scrape together a few dry straws
and spears of grass; the tree-builders, twigs and
lichens and cotton and rootlets and other dry wood

products. There is nothing else for them to use. If a man builds a hut or a shanty in the fields or woods with such material as he finds ready at hand, his habitation will be protectively colored also. The winter wren builds its mouse-like nest of green moss, but in every case that has come under my observation the nest has been absolutely hidden by its position under a log or in a stump, or amid the roots of trees, and the most conspicuous colors would not have betrayed it to its enemies. In fact, the birds that build hidden nests in holes or tree cavities use of necessity the same neutral materials as those that build openly.

Birds that deliberately face the exterior of their nests with lichens obtained from rocks and trees, such as the hummingbird, the blue-gray gnat-catcher, and the wood pewee, can hardly do so with a view to protection, because the material of their nests is already weather-worn and inconspicuous. The lichens certainly give the nest an artistic finish and make it a part of the branch upon which it is placed, to an extent that suggests something like taste in the builders. But I fail to see how a marauding crow, or a jay, or a squirrel, or a weasel, or any other enemy of the bird could be cheated by this device.

IV

I find myself less inclined to look upon the neutral grays and browns of the animal world as the result of the struggle for existence, but more disposed to regard them as the result of the same law or tendency that makes nature in general adaptive and harmonious — the outcome of the blendings, the adjustments, the unifying processes or tendencies that are seen and felt all about us. Is not open-air nature ever striving toward a deeper harmony and unity? Do not differences, discrepancies, antagonisms, tend to disappear? Is there not everywhere something at work to bring about agreements, correspondences, adaptations? to tone down contrasts, to soften outlines, to modify the abrupt, to make peace between opposites? Is not the very condition of life and well-being involved in this principle? The abrupt, the disjoined, the irreconcilable, mean strife and dissolution; while agreements, gradations, easy transitions, mean life and growth. Like tends to beget like; the hand is subdued to the element it works in. The environment sets its stamp more or less strongly upon all living things. Even the pyramids are the color of the sands. Leave your bones there, and they will soon be of the same tint. Even your old boots or old coat will in time come to blend a little with the desert.

The tendency in nature that is over all and under all is the tendency or effort toward harmony — to get rid of strife, discord, violent contrasts, and to adjust every creature to its environment. Inside of this great law or tendency are the lesser laws of change, variety, opposition, contrast. Life must go on, and life for the moment breaks the unity, the balance. May not what is called protective coloration be largely this stamp of the environment, this tendency to oneness, to harmony and simplicity, that pervades nature, organic no less than inorganic?

Things in nature blend and harmonize; one thing matches with another. All open-air objects tend to take on the same color-tones; everything in the woods becomes woodsy, things upon the shore get the imprint of the shore, things in the water assume the hues of the water, the lichen matches the rock and the trees, the shell matches the beach and the waves; everywhere is the tendency to unity and simplicity, to low tones and adaptive colors.

One would not expect animals of the plains or of the desert to be colored like those of the bush or of the woods; the effects of the strong uniform light in the one case and of the broken and checkered light in the other would surely result in different coloration. That never-ending brown or gray or white should not in time stamp itself upon the creatures living in the midst of them is incredible.

Through the action of this principle, water animals will be water-colored, the fish in tropic seas will be more brilliantly colored than those in northern seas, tropical birds and insects will be of gayer

hues than those of the temperate zones, shore birds
will be shore-tinted, Arctic life will blend more or
less with Arctic snows, ground animals will assimi-
late to the ground colors, tree animals will show
greater variety in tint and form, plains animals will
be dull of hue like the plains — all this, as I fancy,
not primarily for protection or concealment, but
through the law of natural assimilation, like begetting like, variety breeding variety.

What more natural than that strictly wood birds
should be of many colors and shades, to be in keeping with their surroundings? Will not the play of
light and shade, the multiplicity of forms, and the
ever moving leaves come in time to have their due
effect? Will not a variety of influences tend to produce a variety of results? Will not sameness breed
sameness? Would not one expect the hummingbirds to be more brilliant than the warblers, and the
warblers more varied in color than the finches?
the insect-feeders than the seed-eaters? The hummingbirds are, as it were, begotten by the flowers
and the sunshine, as the albatross is begotten by
the sea, and the whippoorwill by the dusk. The
rat will not be as bright of tint as the squirrel, nor
the rabbit as the fox.

In the spring one may sometimes see a bluebird,
or a redbird, or a bright warbler for a moment upon
the ground. How artificial and accidental it looks,
like a piece of ribbon or a bit of millinery dropped

there! It is not one with the ground, it is not at
home there. In the tree it is more in keeping with
the changing forms and the sharper contrasts.

The environment is potent in many ways. Everything is modified by the company it keeps. Do not
the quiet tints and sounds of the country have their
effect upon the health and character of the dwellers
there? The citizen differs in look and manner
from the countryman, the lawyer from the preacher
and the doctor, the seaman from the landsman, the
hermit from the cosmopolite. There is the rural
dullness, and there is the metropolitan alertness.
Local color, local quality, are realities. States,
cities, neighborhoods, have shades of difference in
speech and manner. The less traveled a people
are, the more marked these differences appear.
The more a man stays at home, the more the stamp
of his environment is upon him. The more limited
the range of an animal, the more it is modified by
its immediate surroundings. Thus the loon is so
much of a water bird that upon the land it can
only hobble, and the swallow is so much a creature
of the air that its feet are of little use to it. Perfect adaptability usually narrows the range, as the
skater is at home only upon the ice.

Here are two closely related birds of ours, the
oven-bird and the water-thrush, both with speckled
breasts, but each tinted more or less like the ground
it walks upon, the one like the dry leaves, the other

like the brook stones and pond margins. The law of assimilation and of local color has done its perfect work. Were the two birds to change places, each retaining its own color, I do not believe they would be in any more jeopardy than they are now.

The camel is of a uniform gray like the desert where it is at home, while the camelopard, or giraffe, a creature of the trees, is dappled or spotted. Is the color in either case protective? Against what? Their size and movements would disclose them to their natural enemies wherever they were.

The lion is desert-colored too. Is this for concealment from its prey? But it is said that horses and oxen scent the lion long before they can see him, as doubtless do the wild desert creatures upon which he feeds. Their scent would surely be keener than that of our domesticated animals, and to capture them he must run them down or ambush them where the wind favors him. His desert color is the brand of his environment. If his home were the rocks or the mountains, his color would certainly be different. Nothing could be duller or more neutral than the color of the elephant, and surely he is not hiding from any natural enemy, or stalking any game.

The bright colors of many tropical fish, such as the angel-fish, seem only a reflection of the bright element in which they live. The changing brilliant

hues of tropic seas are expressed in the animal life
in them. It is highly improbable that this is for protection; it is the law of assimilation working in the
deep. All life in the tropics is marked by greater
eccentricity of form and richness of coloring than
in the temperate zones, and this is in keeping with
the above principle.

v

It seems to me that the question that enters most
deeply into the life problem of an animal is the
question of food and climate, and of climate only
so far as it affects the food supply. Many of our
migrating birds will brave our northern winters if
they can get anything to eat. A few years ago our
bluebirds in the eastern part of the continent were
fearfully decimated by a cold wave and an ice storm
in the South that cut off their food supply. For two
or three years rarely was a bluebird seen in those
parts of the country where, before that event, they
had been abundant. Then they began to reappear,
and now, it seems to me, there are more bluebirds than ever before. Evidently their bright
colors have not stood in the way of their increase.
If they have now reached their limit, it is because
they have reached the limit of their food supply and
their nesting-sites.

How abundant are the robins everywhere, how
noisy, how conspicuous! I do not doubt in the least

that if, retaining the same habits, they were scarlet, or white, or indigo, they would be just as numerous as they are now. The robin is a wide, free feeder, boring in the turf for grubs and worms in summer, and taking up with cedar berries and hardhack drupes in winter. If a crop of locusts come in cherry time, he will spare your cherries. If a drouth drives the angleworms deep into the ground in August, look out for your grapes. The robin is wonderfully adaptive. If he does not find a tree to his liking, he will nest on the wall, or under your porch, or even on the ground. His colors are not brilliant, but the secret of his success lies in his courage, his force of character, so to speak, and his adaptability. His European cousin, the blackbird, is less protectively colored, but is of similar habits and disposition, and seems to thrive equally well. Again, contrast the Baltimore oriole with the orchard oriole. If there is anything in protective color, the more soberly colored bird has greatly the advantage, and yet the more brilliant species is far more abundant. The strong contrast of black and orange which the brilliant coats present does not seem to have lessened their wearers' chances of survival. Their pendent nests, beyond the reach of weasels and squirrels and snakes and crows, are no doubt greatly in their favor, but still more so, I believe, are their feeding habits. Compared with the orchard oriole, they are miscellaneous feeders; insects and

85

fruit and even green peas are in their bill of fare.
When a bird like the orchard oriole is restricted
in its range, it is quite certain that its food supply
is equally restricted.

Of birds that live upon tree-trunks, here are two
of similar habits, one protectively colored and the
other not, and yet the one that is of bright tints is
far the more numerous. I refer to the nuthatch and
the brown creeper. The creeper is so near the color
of the bark of the trees upon which it feeds that one
has great difficulty in seeing it, while the nuthatch
in its uniform of black, white, and blue, contrasts
strongly with its surroundings. The creeper works
up and around the tree, rarely showing anything
but its bark-colored back, while the nuthatch hops
up and down and around the tree with head lifted,
constantly exposing its white throat and breast.
But the nuthatch is the better feeder, it eats nuts
as well as the larvæ of insects, while the creeper
seems limited to a minute kind of food which it
obtains with that slender, curved bill. It can probe,
but not break, with this instrument, and is never
seen feeding upon the ground, like the nuthatch.
I am bound to state, however, that the latter
bird has another advantage over the demure creeper,
which may offset the danger that might come to
it from its brighter color — it is more supple and
alert. Its contact with the tree is like that of the
rocker with the floor, while the line of the creeper's

back is more like that of the rocker reversed; it
touches head and tail, and has far less freedom of
movement than has the nuthatch. The head of the
latter often points straight out from the tree, and
the eye takes in all the surroundings to an extent
that the creeper's cannot.

Of course it is not safe to claim that one can always put his finger upon the exact thing that makes
one species of birds more numerous than an allied
species; the conditions of all animal life are complex,
and involve many factors more or less obscure.
In the present case I am only trying to point out
how slight a part color seems to play in the problem,
and how prominent a part food plays. Our ruffed
grouse holds its own against the gunners, the trap-
pers, the hard winters, and all its numerous natural
enemies, not, I think, because it is protectively colored, but because it, too, is a miscellaneous feeder,
ranging from berries and insects to buds and leaves.
The quail has the same adaptive coloring, but not
the same range of food supply, and hence is more
easily cut off. Birds that subsist upon a great variety
of foods, no matter what their coloring, apparently
have the best chance of surviving.

VI

There seem to be two instincts in animal life that
work against the influence of environment upon
the colors of animals, or the tendency in Nature to

make her neutral grays and browns everywhere prevail — the male instinct of reproduction, which is major, and the social or gregarious instinct, which is minor, but which, I am inclined to believe, has its effect.

The gregarious birds and mammals are as a rule less locally colored than those of solitary habits. Thus the more gregarious elk and antelope and sheep are less adaptively colored than the more solitary deer. The buffalo had not the usual color of a plains animal; the individual was lost in the mass, and the mass darkened the earth. The musk ox goes in herds and does not put on a white coat in the sub-Arctic regions.

Does a solitary life tend to beget neutral and obscure tints in a bird or beast? The flocking birds nearly all tend to bright colors, at least brighter than their solitary congeners. The passenger pigeon furnished a good example near at hand. Contrast its bright hues with those of the more recluse turtledove. Most of our blackbirds have a strong flocking instinct, and they are conspicuously colored. The sociability of the cedar-birds may help to account for their crests, their banded tails, and their pure, fine browns. As soon as any of the ground birds show a development of the flocking instinct, their hues become more noticeable, as is the case with the junco, the snow bunting, the shore lark, and the lark bunting of the West. Among the tree *Fringil-*

lidæ the same tendency may be noticed, the flocking crossbills, pine grosbeaks, redpolls, and the like, all being brighter of color than the solitary sparrows. The robin is the most social of our thrushes, and is the brightest-colored.

In the tropics the parrots and parrakeets and macaws are all strikingly colored, and are all very social. Why should not this be so? Numbers beget warmth and enthusiasm. A multitude is gay of spirit. It is always more noisy and hilarious, more festive and playful, than are single individuals. Each member is less a part of its surroundings and more a part of the flock or the herd. Its associations with nature are less intimate than with its own kind. Sociability, in the human species, tends to express itself in outward symbols and decorations, and why may not the brighter colors of the social birds be the outward expression of the same spirit?

The social flamingo does not, in the matter of color, seem to have been influenced by its environment at all. The gregarious instinct is evidently very strong in the species. Mr. Frank M. Chapman found them in the Bahamas living and breeding in great colonies; he discovered what he calls a flamingo city. The birds all moved and acted in concert. Their numbers showed in the distance like an army of redcoats; they made the land pink. They were adapted to their marsh life by their long legs, and to the food they ate by their bills, but their colors contrasted strongly with their surroundings. The community spirit carried things with a high hand. The same is in a measure true of the ibis, the stork, the crane — all birds more or less gregarious, and all birds of more or less gay plumes. But our solitary great blue heron, lone watcher in marshes and by pond and river margins, is obscurely colored, as is the equally solitary little green heron.

Our blue heron will stand for hours at a time on the margin of some lake or pond, or on the top of some forest tree near the water, and the eye might easily mistake him for some inanimate object. He has watched among roots and snags and dead tree-tops so long that he has naturally come to look like these things. What his enemies are, that he should need to hide from them, other than the fool with the gun, I do not know.

Among gregarious mammals the same spirit seems at work to check or modify the influence of the environment.

The common crow illustrates this spirit in a wider field. The crow is a citizen of the world; he is at home everywhere, but in the matter of color he is at home nowhere. His jet black gives him away at all times and in all places. His great cunning and suspicion — whence do they come? From his experiences with man?

I do not know that there is very much in this

idea as to the effect of the social instinct upon the colors of animals. I only throw it out as a suggestion.

When we come to the reproductive principle or instinct, then do we strike a dominating influence; then is there contrast and excess and riot; then are there positive colors and showy ornaments; then are there bright flowers, red, orange, white, blue; then are there gaudy plumes of birds, and obtrusive forms and appendages in mammals. The old modesty and moderation of nature are abandoned. It is not now a question of harmony and quietude, but of continuing the species. Masses of color appear in the landscape; silent animals become noisy; birds burst into song, or strut and dance and pose before one another; the marshes are vocal; hawks scream and soar; a kind of madness seizes all forms of life; the quail whistles; the grouse drums in the woods, or booms upon the prairie; the shellfish in the sea, and the dull turtle upon the land, feel the new impulse that thrills through nature. The carnival of the propagating instinct is at hand. For this, and begotten by this, are the gaudy colors and the beautiful and the grotesque ornaments.

As a rule, the females are not implicated in this movement or craze to the extent that the males are. Even among the flowering plants and trees in which the two sexes are separated, the male is showy while the female is inconspicuous. The pollen-yield-

ing catkins of the hazel and of the hickory and
oak flaunt in the wind, seen by all passers, while
the minute fruit-producing flower is seen by none.
Nature always keeps nearer to her low tones, to
her neutral ground, in the female than in the
male; the female is nearer the neuter gender than
is the male. She is negative when he is positive;
she is more like the quiet color tones in nature; she
represents the great home-staying, conservative,
brooding mother principle that pervades the universe. Harmony, repose, flowing lines, subdued
colors, are less the gift of the aggressive, warring
masculine element than of the withdrawing and
gentle feminine element. That the earth is our
mother, the sun our father, is a feeling as old as the
human race, and throughout the animal world the
neutral and negative character of the one and the
color and excess of the other still mark the two
sexes. Why, in the human species, the woman runs
more to the ornate and the superfluous than does the
man is a question which no doubt involves socio-
logical considerations that are foreign to my subject.

Darwin accounts for the wide departure from the
principle of utility and of protective coloration in
the forms and colors of so many birds and mammals
upon his theory of sexual selection, or the preference of the female for bright colors and odd forms.
Wallace rejects this theory, and attributes these
things to the more robust health and vigor of the

males. However, in the matter of health the females of all species seem on a par with the males, though in many cases the males are the larger and the more powerful. But among our familiar birds, when the two sexes differ in color, the brighter-plumaged male, with rare exceptions, is no larger or more vigorous than the female.

The principle to which I have referred seems to me adequate to account for these gay plumes and fantastic forms — the male sexual principle, the positive, aggressive instinct of reproduction, always so much more active in the male than in the female; an instinct or passion that banishes fear, prudence, cunning, that makes the timid bold, the sluggish active, that runs to all sorts of excesses, that sharpens the senses, that quickens the pulse, that holds in abeyance hunger and even the instinct of self-preservation, that arms for battle and sounds forth the call, and sows contention and strife everywhere; the principle that gives the beard to the man, the mane to the lion, the antlers to the stag, the tusks to the elephant, and — why not? — the gorgeous plumes and bright colors to the male birds of so many species. The one thing that Nature seems to have most at heart is reproduction; she will sacrifice almost everything else to this — the species must be perpetuated at all hazards, and she has, as a rule, laid the emphasis in this matter upon the male. The male in the human species is positive,

or plus, while the female is negative. The life of
the female among the lower animals runs more
smoothly and evenly — is more on the order of the
neutral tint — than is that of the male. The females
of the same group differ from one another much
less than do the males. The male carries a com-
mission that makes him more restless, feverish, and
pugnacious. He is literally "spoiling for a fight"
most of the time. This surplusage, these loaded
dice, make the game pretty sure.

Cut off the ugly bull's horns, and you have tamed
him. Castration tames him still more, and changes
his whole growth and development, making him
approximate in form and disposition to the female.
I fancy that the same treatment would have the
same effect upon the peacock, or the bird of para-
dise, or any other bird of fantastic plumage and
high color. Destroy the power of reproduction, and
the whole masculine fabric of pride — prowess,
weapons and badges, gay plumes and decorations
— falls into ruins.

When we remember how inattentive and indifferent the females of all species of birds are to the
displays of the males before them, it is incredible
that their taste in fashions, their preferences for the
gay and the ornate, should have played any con-
siderable part in superinducing these things.

Darwin traces with great skill the gradual development of the ball and socket ocelli in the plumage

of the Argus pheasant. It was evidently a long, slow process. Is it credible that the female observed and appreciated each successive slight change in the growth of these spots, selecting those males in which the changes were most marked, and rejecting the others? How could she be so influenced by changes so slight and so gradual that only a trained eye would be likely to take note of them? It is imputing to the female bird a degree of taste and a power of discrimination that are found only in mankind. Why, then, it may be asked, is the male so active in showing off his finery before the female? Of course it is to move her, to excite her to the point of mating with him. His gay plumes are the badge of his masculinity, and it is to his masculinity that her feminine nature responds. She is aroused when he brings to bear upon her all the batteries of his male sex. She is negative at the start, as he is positive. She must be warmed up, and it is his function to do it. She does not select; she accepts, or rejects. The male does the selecting. He offers himself, and she refuses or agrees, but the initiative is with him always. He would doubtless strut just the same were there no hens about. He struts because he has to, because strutting is the outward expression of his feelings. The presence of the hen no doubt aggravates the feeling, and her response is a reaction to the stimuli he offers, just as his own struttings are reactions to the internal stimuli that are at the

95

time governing him. In the Zoo at the Bronx the peacock has been seen to strut before a crow.

Undoubtedly the males in whom the masculine principle is the strongest and most masterful are most acceptable to the females, and the marvelous development of form and color in the peacock, or in the Argus pheasant, might take place under the stimulus of continued success. If there are two rival cocks in the yard, the hens will, as a rule, prefer the victor — the one that struts the most and crows the loudest. How amusing to see the defeated cock fold his wings, depress his plumage, and look as unpretentious and henlike as possible in the presence of his master!

If the male bird sang only while courting the female, we might think he sang only to excite her admiration, but he continues to sing until the young appear, and, fitfully, long after that, his bright colors in many cases gradually disappearing with his declining song impulse, and both fading out as the sexual instinct has run its course. It was the sexual impulse that called them into being, and they decline as it declines. It is this impulse that makes all male birds so pugnacious during the breeding season. Not only does a brighter iris come upon the burnished dove in the spring, but also a warmer glow comes upon the robin's breast, and the hues of all other male birds are more or less deepened and intensified at this time. Among many kinds of fish the males put on brighter colors in the spring, and surely this cannot be to win the females, as there is no proper mating among them.

The odd forms and bizarre colors that so often prevail among birds, more especially tropical and semi-tropical birds, and among insects, suggest fashions among men, capricious, fantastic, gaudy, often grotesque, and having no direct reference to the needs of the creatures possessing them. They are clearly the riot and overflow of the male sexual principle — the carnival of the nuptial and breeding impulse. The cock or sham nests of the male wrens seem to be the result of the excess and overflow of the same principle.

It is not, therefore, in my view of the case, female selection that gives the males their bright plumage, but the inborn tendency of the masculine principle to riot and overplus. There is, strictly speaking, no wooing, no courtship, among the four-footed beasts, and yet the badges of masculinity, manes, horns, tusks, pride, pugnacity, are as pronounced here as are the male adornments among the fowls of the air.

Why, among the polygamous species of birds, are the males so much more strongly marked than among the monogamous? Why, but as a result of the superabundance and riot of the male sexual principle? In some cases among the quadrupeds it even greatly increases the size of the males over the females, as among the polygamous fur seals.

Darwin came very near to the key of the problem that engaged him, when he said that the reason why the male has been the more modified in those cases where the sexes differ in external appearance is that "the males of almost all animals have stronger passions than the females."

"In mankind, and even as low down in the scale as in the *Lepidoptera*, the temperature of the body is higher in the male than in the female." (Darwin.)

If the female refuses the male, it is not because he does not fill her eye or arouse her admiration, but because the mating instinct is not yet ripe. Among nearly all our birds the males fairly thrust themselves upon the females, and carry them by storm. This may be seen almost any spring day in the squabbles of the English sparrows along the street. The female appears to resist all her suitors, defending herself against them by thrusting spitefully right and left, and just what decides her finally to mate with any one of them is a puzzle. It may be stated as a general rule that all females are reluctant or negative, and all males are eager or positive, and that the male wins, not through the taste of the female, — her love for bright colors and ornamental appendages, — but through the dominance of his own masculinity. He is the stronger force, he is aggressive and persuasive, and finally kindles her with his own breeding instinct.

Even among creatures so low in the scale of life

as the crab, the males of certain species, during the breeding season, dance and gyrate about the females, assuming many grotesque postures and behaving as if intoxicated — as, indeed, they are, with the breeding passion.

Evidently the female crab does not prefer one male over another, but mates with the one that offers himself, as soon as he has excited her to the mating point. And I have no proof that among the birds the female ever shows preference for one male over another; she must be won, of course, and she is won when the male has sufficiently aroused her; she does not choose a mate, but accepts one at the right time. I have seen two male bluebirds fight for hours over a female, while she sat and looked on indifferently. And I have seen two females fight over a male, while he sat and looked on with equal indifference. " Either will suit, but I want but one."

Of course Nature does not work as man works. Our notions of prudence, of precision, of rule and measure, are foreign to her ways. The stakes are hers, whoever wins. She works by no inflexible system or plan, she is spontaneous and variable every moment. She heaps the measure, or she scants the measure, and it is all one to her. Our easy explanations of her ways — how often they leave us where they found us! The balance of life upon the globe is fairly well maintained by checks and counter-checks, by some species being prolific and other species less so, by the development of assimilative colors by one kind, and of showy colors by another, by slow but ceaseless modifications and adaptations. It is a problem of many and complex factors, in which, no doubt, color plays its part, but I believe this part is a minor one.

NOTE. — Since writing the above essay I have read Geddes and Thomson on "The Evolution of Sex," and find that these investigators have anticipated my main idea in regard to the high coloration and ornamentation of male birds, namely that these things inhere in the male principle, or are "natural to maleness." The males put on more beauty than females "because they are males, and not primarily for any other reason whatever." "Bright coloring or rich pigmentation is more characteristic of the male than of the female constitution." "Males are stronger, handsomer, or more emotional simply because they are males, — *i. e.*, of more active physiological habit than their mates." The males tend to live at a loss, and are relatively more *katabolic;* the females, on the other hand, tend to live at a profit, and are relatively more *anabolic*.

"Brilliancy of color, exuberance of hair and feathers, activity of scent-glands, and even the development of weapons, cannot be satisfactorily explained by sexual selection alone, for this is merely a secondary factor. In origin and continued development they are outcrops of a male as opposed to a female constitution."

VI

STRAIGHT SEEING AND STRAIGHT THINKING

I

A NEWSPAPER correspondent the other day asked me what I meant by truth in natural history. "We know that no two persons see alike," he said, "or see the same things; behold the disagreements in the testimony of eye-witnesses to the same occurrences." "True," I replied; "but when two persons shoot at a mark, they must see alike if they are both to hit the mark, and two witnesses to a murder or a robbery must agree substantially in their testimony if they expect to be credited in the court-room." In like manner, two observers in the field of natural history must in the main agree in their statements of fact if their observations are to have any scientific value. Notwithstanding it is true that we do not all see the same things when we go to the fields and woods, there is such a thing as accurate seeing, and there is such a thing as inaccurate seeing and reporting.

By truth in natural history I can mean only that which is verifiable; that which others may see under like conditions, or which accords with the observa-

tions of others. You may not see just what I do in
the lives of the birds or the quadrupeds, but you
will see that which belongs to the same order of
facts, just as you will in the world of physics. You
will not see iron floating and wood sinking under
like conditions, or trees growing with their roots in
the air. You may see to-day something in the life
of a bird, or a bee, or a beast, that neither I nor
any one else ever saw before, but it will belong to
the same order of things that I and others have
seen these creatures do. You will not see a woodchuck hanging to a limb by his tail like a possum,
nor a fox sleeping in the top of a tree like a coon,
nor a loon running a race between lines of interested spectators, nor crows hoarding trinkets in
a hollow stump, nor the old teaching their young
this or that, and so on. No, you may send a thousand good observers to the woods every day for
a thousand years, and not one of them will see any
of the novel and surprising, not to say impossible,
things of which the "nature fakers" see so many
every time they take a walk. The nature faker's
fantastic natural history is not verifiable. I have
seen blackbirds build their nests in the side of an osprey's nest, and all seemed to go well — the osprey
is exclusively a fish-eater — but if any person were
to tell me that he had seen them build their nests
alongside of that of the eagle or the hen-hawk, or
that he had seen bluebirds breeding in a cavity with

102

the hoot owl, I should know him as a faker. The rabbit is not on visiting terms with the fox or the mink, nor do the robins welcome a call from the jays.

I did something the other day with a wild animal that I had never done before or seen done, though I had heard of it: I carried a live skunk by the tail, and there was "nothing doing," as the boys say. I did not have to bury my clothes. I knew from observation that the skunk could not use its battery with effect without throwing its tail over its back; therefore, for once at least, I had the courage of my convictions and verified the fact.

A great many intelligent persons tolerate or encourage our fake natural history on the ground that they find it entertaining, and that it interests the school-children in the wild life about them. Is the truth, then, without value for its own sake? What would these good people think of a United States school history that took the same liberties with facts that certain of our nature writers do: that, for instance, made Washington take his army over the Delaware in balloons, or in sleighs on the solid ice with bands playing; or that made Lincoln a victim of the Evil Eye; or that portrayed his slayer as a self-sacrificing hero; or that represented the little Monitor that eventful day on Hampton Roads as diving under the Merrimac and tossing it ashore on its beak?

The nature fakers take just this kind of liberties with the facts of our natural history. The young reader finds it entertaining, no doubt, but is this sufficient justification?

Again, I am told that the extravagant stories of our wild life are or may be true from the writer's point of view. One of our publishing houses once took me to task for criticising the statements of one of its authors by charging that I had not considered his point of view. The fact is, I had considered it too well; his point of view was that of the man who tells what is not so. As if there could be more than one legitimate point of view in natural history observation — the point of view of fact!

There is a great deal of loose thinking upon this subject in the public mind.

An editorial writer in a New England newspaper, defending this school of writers, says:—

"Their point of view is that of the great out-of-doors, and comes from loving sympathy with the life they study, and is as different from that of the sportsman and the laboratory zoölogist as a note-book differs from a rifle or a microscope."

Now how the point of view of the "great out-of-doors" can differ from the point of view of the little indoors in regard to matters of fact is hard to see. A man who watches the ways of an animal in the wilderness, or from the mountain-top, is bound by the same laws of truthfulness as the man who sees

104

A Skunk

it through his study window. What the writer means is doubtless that the spirit in which the literary naturalist — the man who goes to the fields and woods for material for literature — treats the facts of natural history differs from the spirit in which the man of pure science treats his. Undoubtedly, but the two alike deal with facts, though with facts of a different order.

The scientist, the artist, the nature-lover, and the like, all look for and find different things in nature, yet there is no contradiction between the different things they find. The truth of one is not the falsehood of another. The field naturalist is interested in the live animal, the laboratory zoölogist in the measuring and dissecting of the dead carcass. What interests one is of little or no interest to the other. So with the field botanist as compared with the mere herbalist. Both are seekers for the truth, but for a different kind of truth. One seeks that kind of truth that appeals to his emotion and to his imagination; the other that kind of truth — truth of structure, relation of parts, family ties — that appeals to his scientific faculties. Does this fact, therefore, give the nature faker warrant to exaggerate or to falsify the things he sees in the fields and woods? Let him make the most of what he sees, embellish it, amplify it, twirl it on the point of his pen like a juggler, but let him beware of adding to it; let him be sure he sees accurately. Let him beware of letting invention take the place of observation. It is one thing to work your gold or silver up into sparkling ornaments, and quite another to manufacture an imitation gold or silver, and this is what the nature fakers do. Their natural history is for the most part a sham, a counterfeit. No one quarrels with them because they are not scientific, or because they deal in something more than dry facts; the ground of quarrel is that they do not start with facts, that they grossly and absurdly misrepresent the wild lives they claim to portray.

A Wisconsin editor, writing upon this subject, shoots wide of the mark in the same way as does the New England editor. "Knowledge born of scientific curiosity," he says, "has nothing in common with the study of animal individuality which the 'nature fakers' have fostered and to which the public has proved responsive. There is all the difference in the world between being interested in the length of an animal's skull and being interested in the same animal's ways and personality." True enough, but this is quite beside the mark. The point at issue is a question of accurate seeing and reporting. The man who is reporting upon an animal's ways and personality is bound by the same obligations of truthfulness as the man who is occupied with the measurements of its skull. By all means let the literary naturalist give us traits instead of measurements. This he is bound to do, and the better he does it, the better we shall like him. We can get our statistics elsewhere. From him we want pictures, action, incident, and the portrait of the living animal. But we want it all truthfully done. The life history of any of our wild creatures, the daily and hourly course of its life, all its traits and peculiarities, all its adventures and ways of getting on in the world, are of keen interest to every nature student, but if these things are misrepresented, what then? There are readers, I believe, who say they don't care whether the thing is true or not; at any rate it is interesting, and that is enough. What can one say to such readers? Only that they should not complain if they are *stuck* with paste diamonds, or pinchbeck gold, or shoddy cloth, or counterfeit bills.

The truth of animal life is more interesting than any fiction about it. Can there be any doubt, for instance, that if one knew just how the fur seals find their way back from the vast wilderness of the Pacific Ocean, where there is, apparently, nothing for the eye, or the ear, or the nose to seize upon in guiding them, to the little island in Bering Sea that is their breeding haunt in spring — can there be any doubt, I say, that such knowledge would be vastly more interesting than anything our natural history romancers could invent about it? But it is the way of our romancers to draw upon their invention when their observation fails them. Thus one of them tells how the salmon get up the high falls that they meet with in the rivers they ascend in spring — it is by easy stages; they rest upon shelves or upon niches in the rocks behind the curtain of water, and leap from these upward through the pouring current till the top is gained; and he tells it as if he knew it to be a fact, when, in truth, it is a fiction.

Then this so-called individuality of the animals is enormously exaggerated by the nature fakers. The difference between two individuals of the same species in a wild state is but a small matter. What is true of one is practically true of all the others. They are all subject to the same conditions, and the life problems are essentially the same with each; hence their variations are but slight, while in the case of man the variations are enormous. One child is born a genius and another is born a dunce. The mass of mankind would still be sunk in barbarism had it not been for the few superior minds born in every age and country, who have lifted the standard of living and thinking to a higher plane. It is only when the lower animals are brought in contact with man and subjected to artificial conditions that wide diversity of character and disposition appears among them. Then we have on the farm the bucking horse, the intractable ox, the unruly cow, and, in the circus, the trained lion or tiger or elephant that suddenly "goes bad." In domestication the difference in the disposition of squirrels, foxes, ,coons, and other animals comes out, but in the wild state their habits and traits are practically all the same. A fox hunter who knows his territory well will point out to you the course all foxes when pursued by the hounds are very likely to take, generation after generation; the conformation of the land determining the course. Rarely does the fox run wild and upset the calculations of the hunter. But the differences between the behavior of hunted animals under like conditions is not, I think, an evidence of original traits and dispositions in the hunted. One grizzly, or one moose, or one wild boar will charge you when wounded, and another will run away. So will one stick of dynamite explode in the handling while others remain inert; so will one swarm of bees be ugly to-day and docile to-morrow. Slight differences in external conditions, no doubt, determine the result in each case.

I see the herring gulls flying up the river above the floating ice, as I write. Now all those gulls may not be absolutely alike to the last feather, but they are as nearly alike in character as the fragments of floating ice are alike in character. I would not dare affirm any trait or characteristic of one that I would not affirm of all the others. And the score or more of crows perched upon the ice beneath them — what one of those crows will do in its wild state, each and every other crow will or may do. There are no

geniuses or heroes among them. Hence when our
nature fakers claim that they study individuals and
not species, they need watching. Let them exploit
the individual certainly, but let them be cautious
how they claim exceptional traits or intelligence
for it.

Let me return to the editors. One of our most
influential weekly journals, in defending the nature
fakers against the attack of President Roosevelt,
makes this statement: —

"We quite agree that fiction ought not to be
palmed off on school-children as fact; but we do
not agree with what is implied, that imagination
may not be used in interpreting and narrating facts.
Men see through their temperaments; the imaginative man sees through his imagination, and he is
telling the truth if he tells what he sees as he sees it.
Mr. Froude, who had a vivid historical imagination,
was bitterly condemned by Mr. Freeman, who had
none; but Mr. Froude's history is not only interesting, while Mr. Freeman's is dull, but very eminent
authorities regard him as the better historian of the
two."

Behold what confusion of thought there is in this
paragraph. The writer confounds the interpretation of facts with the observation of facts; he
confounds the world of ideas with the world of
concrete experiences; he confounds the historian of
human annals with the eye-witness of daily events in

the lives of our wild creatures. Neither Froude nor Freeman wrote from observation or experience, as our nature fakers claim to, but from the study of past men and events as recorded by others. They were interpreting the records, and their temperaments and imaginations greatly modified the results. But other things being equal, would we not prefer the historian who kept closest to the record, to the actual facts, of the case? Truthfulness is a merit, imagination is a merit, and neither can take the place of the other. When the two are combined, we get the best results.

Truth in natural history is much easier to reach than truth in civil history. Civil history is vastly more complex. Moreover, it is of the past in a sense that the other is not, and the writers of it are rarely the eye-witnesses of the events they describe; while natural history is being daily and hourly enacted all around us, and varies but little from year to year. A truthful account of the life history of one animal holds substantially correct for all the rest of that species in different places and times. The animal is a part of its environment, and has no independent history in the sense that a man has.

Certainly " the imagination may be used in interpreting and narrating facts " — must be used, if anything of literary value is to be the outcome. But it is one thing to treat your facts with imagination and quite another to imagine your facts. So long as the natural historian or the human historian is sound upon his facts, we know where we stand. But the faker is a faker because he disregards the facts. Froude uses more imagination in dealing with his material than Freeman did, hence he has much greater charm and power of style. It is only when he disregards the fact, or takes unwarranted liberties with it, that Freeman can justly criticise him.

There has been no such luminous interpreter of the facts of natural history as Darwin; he read their meaning as no one else had ever before done. His reason and his imagination went hand in hand. But was there ever a mind more loyal to the exact truth? Every man who brought him a fact brought him material for the edifice he was so intent upon building — an edifice which the human mind since his day is dwelling in with more and more contentment.

It is in the interpretation of natural facts and phenomena that temperament, imagination, emotional sensibility, come in play. In all subjective fields — in religion, politics, art, philosophy — one man's truth may be another man's falsehood, but in the actual concrete world of observation and experience, if we all see correctly, we shall all see alike. Blue is blue and red is red, and our colorblindness does not alter the fact. In emotional and imaginative fields a man may be "telling the truth if he tells what he sees as he sees it," but in the field of actual observation he is telling the truth only when he tells the thing as it really is, reports the habits and behavior of the animals as they really are. What do we mean by powers of observation but the power to see the thing as it is — to see the truth? An opulent imagination cannot make up for feeble powers of observation. The effect the fact observed has upon you, what you make of it, what it signifies to you — that is another matter. Here interpretation comes in, and on this line you have the field all to yourself. I may think your interpretation absurd, but I shall not question your veracity or honesty of purpose. We are very likely to differ in taste, in opinions about this and that, in religion, politics, art, but we must agree upon facts. Unless there is some chance that men can see and report accurately, what becomes of the value of human testimony as given by eye-witnesses on the witness stand? Things do fall out so and so, or they fall out otherwise; it is not a matter of imagination or of temperament in the beholder, but a matter of accurate seeing. In getting at the value of a man's testimony we may have to take into account his excitable or his phlegmatic temperament and the seductive power of his imagination, and eliminate them as so much dross in a metal. Eye-witnesses generally differ; we must reconcile the differences and sift out the facts.

The animal-story writers, such as Mr. Roberts

and Mr. Seton, aim to give the charm of art and literature to their natural-history lore; so to work up their facts that they appeal to our emotion and imagination. This is legitimate and a high calling, provided they do not transgress the rule I have been laying down, which Mr. Roberts does when he represents the skunk as advertising his course through the woods to all other creatures by his characteristic odor, since the skunk emits that odor only when attacked, and is at all other times as odorless as a squirrel; or when he says the fox is too cunning to raid the poultry yard near its own door, but will go far off for its plunder. I wish the pair of foxes that had their den within easy rifle-shot of our farmhouse the past season had acted upon this policy. We should have reared more chickens, and one of the foxes would not have met his death in a charge of shot as he did while he was chasing a hen through the currant patch in broad daylight.

The principal aim of the teacher of nature study in the schools should be to help the children to see straight, to develop and sharpen their powers of observation, and to give them rational views of animal mentality.

When one of our nature writers, whose methods have been much criticised, says in the introduction to one of his books on animal life that he would " make nature study more vital and attractive by

114

revealing a vast realm of nature outside the realm of science," is not one set to puzzling one's brain as to how there can be any legitimate nature study that will carry one beyond the realm of science? Is there any subject-matter in the books thus prefaced that science cannot deal with? And why does the author aver with such emphasis that his facts are all true and verifiable? — just the test that science demands. If it is all true and sound natural history, what puts it outside the realm of science? If it is not true and real, why call it nature study? Why not call it the gentle art of bearing false witness against the animals? But this realm of nature outside the realm of science — the realm of the occult — is not open to observation, and is therefore not a subject for nature study. The realm of science embraces the whole visible, tangible, and intangible universe. Is not that field enough for nature study? Can there be any other field? What lies outside of this is mere matter of speculation.

The works of the writer referred to are outside the realm of science only as every exaggeration and falsification is outside that realm, or as Alice in Wonderland and Jack and his beanstalk are outside. Such a course may make nature study more attractive to certain credulous minds, but it can hardly make it more vital, or add to our knowledge of the world and its denizens by which we are surrounded.

II

To see accurately and completely is a power given to few; hence the observations of the majority of people are of no scientific value whatever. One spring I was interested in the question as to how the crow picks up a dead fish or other food from the surface of the water — with its feet or its bill. One would naturally say with its bill, of course, as all except the rapacious birds hold and carry things in their beaks. But one of our younger nature writers made the crow carry food for its young in its claws, and a teacher of zoölogy in a Western academy wrote that he had seen a crow pick up a dead fish from a pond and carry it ashore with its feet. I wrote and cross-questioned the teacher a little; among other things, I asked him if he had the point in question in mind when he saw the crow pick up the fish. As I never received an answer, I concluded that this witness broke down on the cross-examination.

I put the question to fishermen on the river: Had they ever seen a crow pick up anything from the surface of the water? Oh, yes, lots of times. Did he seize the object with his feet or his beak? They would pause and think, and then some would reply, "Indeed, I can't say; I did not notice." One man said emphatically, "With his feet;" another was quite as sure it was done with the bill.

I myself was sure I had seen crows pick up food from the water, as gulls do, with the bill. I had the vision of that low stooping of the head while the bird was in the act. I asked my son, who spends much time on the river, and who is a keen observer. He had often seen the thing done, but was not certain whether it was with the beak or the feet. A few days later he was on the river, and saw a crow that had spied a fragment of a loaf of bread floating on the water. Having the point in mind, he watched the crow attentively. Down came old crow with extended legs, and my son said to himself, "Yes, he is going to seize it with his feet." But he did not; his legs went down into the water, for what purpose I cannot say, but he seized the bread with his beak, rose up with it and then dropped it, then seized it again in the same way and bore it toward a tree on the shore. Not many days later I saw a crow pick up something from the river in the same way: the feet went into the water, but the object was seized with the beak. The crow's feet are not talons, and are adapted only to perching and walking. So far as I know, all our birds, except birds of prey, carry their food and their nesting-material in their beaks.

One day I saw an eagle flying over with something like a rope dangling from its feet, probably a black snake. A bird carries its capture with the member by which it seizes it, which with birds of prey is the foot, and with other birds the beak. The kingfisher lives upon fish, and he always seizes them with his beak and swallows them head foremost.

Any testimony the value of which depends upon accuracy in seeing needs to be well sifted, so few persons see straight and see whole. They see a part, and then guess or fancy the rest. I have read that the Scotch fishermen will tell you that the loon carries its egg under its wing till it hatches. One would say they are in a position to know; their occupations bring them often into the haunts of the loon; yet the notion is entirely erroneous. The loon builds a nest and incubates its eggs upon the ground as surely as does the goose or duck.

Not till the mind is purged of dread, superstition, and all notions of a partnership between the visible and the occult will the eye see straight. The mind that is athirst for the marvelous and the mysterious will rarely see straight. The mind that believes the wild creatures are half human, that they plot and plan and reason as men do, will not see straight, or report the facts without addition or diminution. There is plenty that is curious and inexplicable in nature, things that astonish or baffle us, but there is no "hocus-pocus," nothing that moves on the border-land between the known and the unknown, or that justifies the curious superstitions of the past. Things of the twilight are more elusive and difficult of verification than things of the noon, but they are no less real, and no less a part of the common day.

STRAIGHT SEEING AND THINKING

I was reminded of this lately on hearing the twilight flight song of the woodcock — one of the most curious and tantalizing yet interesting bird songs we have. I fancy that the persons who hear and recognize it in the April or May twilight are few and far between. I myself have heard it only on three occasions — one season in late March, one season in April, and the last time in the middle of May. It is a voice of ecstatic song coming down from the upper air and through the mist and the darkness — the spirit of the swamp and the marsh climbing heavenward and pouring out its joy in a wild burst of lyric melody; a haunter of the muck and a prober of the mud suddenly transformed into a bird that soars and circles and warbles like a lark hidden or half hidden in the depths of the twilight sky. The passion of the spring has few more pleasing exemplars. The madness of the season, the abandon of the mating instinct, is in every move and note. Ordinarily the woodcock is a very dull, stupid bird, with a look almost idiotic, and is seldom seen except by the sportsman or the tramper along marshy brooks. But for a brief season in his life he is an inspired creature, a winged song that baffles the eye and thrills the ear from the mystic regions of the upper air.

When I last heard it, I was with a companion, and our attention was arrested, as we were skirting the edge of a sloping, rather marshy, bowlder-strewn field, by the "zeep," "zeep," which the bird utters on the ground, preliminary to its lark-like flight. We paused and listened. The light of day was fast failing; a faint murmur went up from the fields below us that defined itself now and then in the good-night song of some bird. Now it was the lullaby of the song sparrow or the swamp sparrow. Once the tender, ringing, infantile voice of the bush sparrow stood out vividly for a moment on that great back-ground of silence. "Zeep," "zeep," came out of the dimness six or eight rods away. Presently there was a faint, rapid whistling of wings, and my companion said: "There, he is up." The ear could trace his flight, but not the eye. In less than a minute the straining ear failed to catch any sound, and we knew he had reached his climax and was circling. Once we distinctly saw him whirling far above us. Then he was lost in the obscurity, and in a few seconds there rained down upon us the notes of his ecstatic song — a novel kind of hurried, chirping, smacking war-ble. It was very brief, and when it ceased, we knew the bird was dropping plummet-like to the earth. In half a minute or less his "zeep," "zeep," came up again from the ground. In two or three minutes he repeated his flight and song, and thus kept it up during the half-hour or more that we remained to listen: now a harsh plaint out of the obscurity upon the ground; then a jubilant strain from out the obscurity of the air above. His mate was probably somewhere within earshot, and we wondered just how much interest she took in the performance. Was it all for her benefit, or inspired by her presence? I think, rather, it was inspired by the May night, by the springing grass, by the unfolding leaves, by the apple bloom, by the passion of joy and love that thrills through nature at this season. An hour or two before, we had seen the bobolinks in the meadow beating the air with the same excited wing and overflowing with the same ecstasy of song, but their demure, retiring, and indifferent mates were nowhere to be seen. It would seem as if the male bird sang, not to win his mate, but to celebrate the winning, to invoke the young who are not yet born, and to express the joy of love which is at the heart of nature.

When I reached home, I went over the fourteen volumes of Thoreau's Journal to see if he had made any record of having heard the "woodcock's evening hymn," as Emerson calls it. He had not. Evidently he never heard it, which is the more surprising as he was abroad in the fields and marshes and woods at almost all hours in the twenty-four and in all seasons and weathers, making it the business of his life to see and record what was going on in nature.

Thoreau's eye was much more reliable than his ear. He saw straight, but did not always hear straight. For instance, he seems always to have

confounded the song of the hermit thrush with that
of the wood thrush. He records having heard the
latter even in April, but never the former. In the
Maine woods and on Monadnock it is always the
wood thrush which he hears, and never the hermit.

But if Thoreau's ear was sometimes at fault, I
do not recall that his eye ever was, while his mind
was always honest. He had an instinct for the truth,
and while we may admit that the truth he was in
quest of in nature was not always scientific truth, or
the truth of natural history, but was often the truth
of the poet and the mystic, yet he was very careful
about his facts; he liked to be able to make an
exact statement, to clinch his observations by going
again and again to the spot. He never taxes your
credulity. He had never been bitten by the mad
dog of sensationalism that has bitten certain of our
later nature writers.

Thoreau made no effort to humanize the animals.
What he aimed mainly to do was to invest his account of them with literary charm, not by imputing
to them impossible things, but by describing them
in a way impossible to a less poetic nature. The
novel and the surprising are not in the act of the
bird or beast itself, but in Thoreau's way of telling
what it did. To draw upon your imagination for
your facts is one thing; to draw upon your imagination in describing what you see is quite another.
The new school of nature writers will afford many

samples of the former method; read Thoreau's description of the wood thrush's song or the bobolink's song, or his account of wild apples, or of his life at Walden Pond, or almost any other bit of his writing, for a sample of the latter. In his best work he uses language in the imaginative way of the poet.

Literature and science do not differ in matters of fact, but in spirit and method. There is no live literature without a play of personality, and there is no exact science without the clear, white light of the understanding. What we want, and have a right to expect, of the literary naturalist is that his statement shall have both truth and charm, but we do not want the charm at the expense of the truth. I may invest the commonest fact I observe in the fields or by the roadside with the air of romance, if I can, but I am not to put the romance in place of the fact. If you romance about the animals, you must do so unequivocally, as Kipling does and as Æsop did; the fiction must declare itself at once, or the work is vicious. To make literature out of natural history observation is not to pervert or distort the facts, or to draw the long bow at all; it is to see the facts in their true relations and proportions and with honest emotion.

Truth of seeing and truth of feeling are the main requisite: add truth of style, and the thing is done.

VII

HUMAN TRAITS IN THE ANIMALS

THAT there is a deal of human nature in the lower animals is a very obvious fact; or we may turn the proposition around and say, with equal truth, that there is a deal of animal nature in us humans. If man is of animal origin, as we are now all coming to believe, how could this be otherwise? We are all made of one stuff, the functions of our bodies are practically the same, and the workings of our instincts and our emotional and involuntary natures are in many ways identical. I am not now thinking of any part or lot which the lower orders may have in our intellectual or moral life, a point upon which, as my reader may know, I diverge from the popular conception of these matters, but of the extent in which they share with us the ground or basement story of the house of life — certain fundamental traits, instincts, and blind gropings.

Man is a bundle of instincts, impulses, predilections, race and family affinities, and antagonisms, supplemented by the gift of reason — a gift of which he sometimes makes use. The animal is a bundle of instincts, impulses, affinities, appetites, and race traits, without the extra gift of reason.

The animal has sensation, perception, and power of association, and these suffice it. Man has sensation, perception, memory, comparison, ideality, judgment, and the like, which suffice him.

There can be no dispute, I suppose, as to certain emotions and impulses being exclusively human, such as awe, veneration, humility, reverence, self-sacrifice, shame, modesty, and many others that are characteristic of what we call our moral nature. Then there are certain others that we share with our dumb neighbors — curiosity, jealousy, joy, anger, sex love, the maternal and paternal instinct, the instinct of fear, of self-preservation, and so forth.

There is at least one instinct or faculty that the animals have far more fully developed than we have — the homing instinct, which seems to imply a sense of direction that we have not. We have lost it because we have other faculties to take its place, just as we have lost that acute sense of smell that is so marvelously developed in many of the four-footed creatures. It has long been a contention of mine that the animals all possess the knowledge and intelligence which is necessary to their self-preservation and the perpetuity of the species, and that is about all. This homing instinct seems to be one of the special powers that the animals cannot get along without. If the solitary wasp, for instance,

could not find her way back to that minute spot in
the field where her nest is made, a feat quite impossible to you or me, so indistinguishable to our
eye is that square inch of ground in which her hole
is made; or if the fur seal could not in spring re-
trace its course to the islands upon which it breeds,
through a thousand leagues of pathless sea water,
how soon the tribe of each would perish!

The animal is, like the skater, a marvel of skill in
one field or element, or in certain fixed conditions,
while man's varied but less specialized powers
make him at home in many fields. Some of the animals outsee man, outsmell him, outhear him, outrun him, outswim him, because their lives depend
more upon these special powers than his does; but
he can outwit them all because he has the resourcefulness of reason, and is at home in many different
fields. The condor " houses herself with the sky"
that she may have a high point of observation for
the exercise of that marvelous power of vision. An
object in the landscape beneath that would escape
the human eye is revealed to the soaring buzzard.
It stands these birds in hand to see thus sharply;
their dinner depends upon it. If mine depended
upon such powers of vision, in the course of time
I might come to possess it. I am not certain but
that we have lost another power that I suspect the
lower animals possess — something analogous to, or
identical with, what we call telepathy — power to

communicate without words, or signs, or signals. There are many things in animal life, such as the precise concert of action among flocks of birds and fishes and insects, and, at times, the unity of impulse among land animals, that give support to the notion that the wild creatures in some way come to share one another's mental or emotional states to a degree and in a way that we know little or nothing of. It seems important to their well-being that they should have such a gift — something to make good to them the want of language and mental concepts, and insure unity of action in the tribe. Their seasonal migrations from one part of the country to another are no doubt the promptings of an inborn instinct called into action in all by the recurrence of the same outward conditions; but the movements of the flock or the school seem to imply a common impulse that is awakened on the instant in each member of the flock. The animals have no systems or methods in the sense that we have, but like conditions with them always awaken like impulses, and unity of action is reached without outward communication.

The lower animals seem to have certain of our foibles, and antagonisms, and unreasoning petulancies. I was reminded of this in reading the story President Roosevelt tells of a Colorado bear he once watched at close quarters. The bear was fussing around a carcass of a deer, preparatory to burying

128

it. "Once the bear lost his grip and rolled over during the course of some movement, and this made him angry and he struck the carcass a savage whack, just as a pettish child will strike a table against which it has knocked itself." Who does not recognize that trait in himself: the disposition to vent one's anger upon inanimate things — upon his hat, for instance, when the wind snatches it off his head and drops it in the mud or leads him a chase for it across the street; or upon the stick that tripped him up, or the beam against which he bumped his head? We do not all carry our anger so far as did a little three-year-old maiden I heard of, who, on tripping over the rockers of her chair, promptly picked herself up, and carrying the chair to a closet, pushed it in and spitefully shut the door on it, leaving it alone in the dark to repent its wrong-doing.

Our blind, unreasoning animal anger is excited by whatever opposes or baffles us. Of course, when we yield to the anger, we do not act as reasonable beings, but as the unreasoning animals. It is hard for one to control this feeling when the opposition comes from some living creature, as a balky horse or a kicking cow, or a pig that will not be driven through the open gate. When I was a boy, I once saw one of my uncles kick a hive of bees off the stand and halfway across the yard, because the bees stung him when he was about to "take them up." I confess to a fair share of this petulant, un-reasoning animal or human trait, whichever it may be, myself. It is difficult for me to refrain from jumping upon my hat when, in my pursuit of it across the street, it has escaped me two or three times just as I was about to put my hand upon it, and as for a balky horse or a kicking cow, I never could trust myself to deal reasonably with them. Follow this feeling back a few thousand years, and we reach the time when our forbears looked upon all the forces in nature as in league against them. The anger of the gods as shown in storms and winds and pesti-lence and defeat is a phase of the same feeling. A wild animal caught in a steel trap vents its wrath upon the bushes and sticks and trees and rocks within its reach. Something is to blame, something baffles it and gives it pain, and its teeth and claws seek every near object. Of course it is a blind manifestation of the instinct of self-defense, just as was my uncle's act when he kicked over his bee-hive, or as is the angler's impatience when his line gets tangled and his hook gets fast. If the Colorado bear caught his fish with a hook and line, how many times would he lose his temper during the day!

I do not think many animals show their kinship to us by exhibiting the trait I am here discussing. Probably birds do not show it at all. I have seen a nest-building robin baffled and delayed, day after day, by the wind that swept away the straws and rubbish she carried to the top of a timber under my porch. But she did not seem to lose her temper. She did not spitefully reclaim the straws and strings that would persist in falling to the porch floors, but cheerfully went away in search of more. So I have seen a wood thrush time after time carrying the same piece of paper to a branch from which the breeze dislodged it, without any evidence of impatience. It is true that when a string or a horsehair which a bird is carrying to its nest gets caught in a branch, the bird tugs at it again and again to free it from entanglement, but I have never seen any evidence of impatience or spite against branch or string, as would be pretty sure to be the case did my string show such a spirit of perversity. Why your dog bites the stone which you roll for him when he has found it, or gnaws the stick you throw, is not quite clear, unless it be from the instinct of his primitive ancestors to bite and kill the game run down in the chase. Or is the dog trying to punish the stick or stone because it will not roll or fly for him? The dog is often quick to resent a kick, be it from man or beast, but I have never known him to show anger at the door that slammed to and hit him. Probably, if the door held him by his tail or his limb, it would quickly receive the imprint of his teeth.

In reading Bostock on the "Training of Wild Animals," my attention was arrested by the remark that his performing lions and tigers are liable to suffer from " stage fright," like ordinary mortals, but that "once thoroughly accustomed to the stage, they seem to find in it a sort of intoxication well known to a species higher in the order of nature;" and furthermore, that "nearly all trainers assert that animals are affected by the attitude of an audience, that they are stimulated by the applause of an enthusiastic house, and perform indifferently before a cold audience." If all this is not mere fancy, but is really a fact capable of verification, it shows another human trait in animals that one would not expect to find there. Bears seem to show more human nature than most other animals. Bostock says that they evidently love to show off before an audience: "The conceit and good opinion of themselves, which some performing bears have, is absolutely ridiculous." A trainer once trained a young bear to climb a ladder and set free the American flag, and so proud did the bear become of his accomplishment, that whenever any one was looking on he would go through the whole performance by himself, "evidently simply for the pleasure of doing it." Of course there is room for much fancy here on the part of the spectator, but bears are in so many ways — in their play, in their boxing, in their walking — such grotesque parodies of man, that one is induced to accept the trainer's statements as containing a measure of truth.

A Trained Bear

HUMAN TRAITS IN THE ANIMALS

The preëminent danger of the animal trainer comes under the same conditions that it would probably come to him were he a trainer of wild men, to wit, when he stumbles or falls. In such a case, the lion or tiger is very apt to spring upon him. These beasts seem to know that a man is less formidable when down than when standing; when prone upon the ground, his power has departed. They also, like the human savage, often seize the opportunity for an attack upon him when his back is turned. A bold, threatening front cows an animal as it cows a man. The least sign of fear or of hesitation on the part of the trainer, and he is in danger. Self-confidence, self-control, an authoritative manner, count for just as much in our dealing with the animals as with men. How a bold, unhesitating manner will carry you through a pack of threatening dogs, while timidity or parleying endangers your calves! Act as though you were the rightful master of the place and had come to give orders, and the most threatening watch-dog gives way. Flee from a mad bull, a cross dog, a butting sheep, and your danger is vastly increased. Even an insolent rooster or a bellicose gander will strike you then. I have found that the best way to deal with the hive bee is by a bold and decisive manner. I would even recommend the same course with yellow-jackets; if you are bent on demolishing their nest, do it by a sudden bold stroke, and not by timid approaches.

All kinds of bees seem disconcerted by a sudden onslaught.

Another human trait that seems almost universal among the lower animals is the coyness and reluctance of the female in her relations to the male. Her first impulse is to refuse and to flee. She is negative as the male is positive. Among the birds there is something like regular courtship, there is rivalry and jealousy and hostile collision on the part of both sexes. With the birds, the propagating instinct in the female is evidently not subject to the same law of recurring intervals that it is among mammals. Hence the female must be stimulated and won by the male. He addresses himself to her in a way that is quite exceptional, if it occurs at all, among mammals. His aim seems to be to kindle or quicken her sexual and mating impulses. In the case of mammals, these impulses recur at certain periods, and no courtship on the part of the male is necessary.

Just what part the gay plumes and the extra appendages of the males play in bird courtship I have discussed elsewhere. I think it is highly probable that the bright colors and ornamental plumes of the male react upon him, excite him, and increase his pride, his courage, and the impetuosity of his address. The birds that dance and perform before the females, during the breeding season, seem to show more and more excitement as the dance proceeds, apparently intoxicated by their own ardor. Just what determines the choice of the male and sets him in pursuit of a particular female is a question that greatly interests me. Does the matter turn upon some complementary variation too subtle for us to perceive? The mating of birds certainly seems like an act of choice; but just what determines it, how shall we find that out? Behold the sparrows in the street, three or four males apparently in a scrimmage with one female, surrounding her and playfully assaulting her, with spread plumage and animated chirping and chattering, while she, the centre of the group, strikes right and left, in a serious, angry mood, at her would-be suitors. What does it mean? Or, the robins in the spring, rushing across the lawn and forming sudden rough-and-tumble groups with a struggling and indignant female in the centre, or gleefully screaming, and quickly and apparently amicably separating? In all such cases the hen bird alone wears an angry and insulted air. What indignity has been put upon her? I know of nothing in human courtship analogous to this tumultuous and hilarious pursuit of the females by the cock sparrows and robins.

The gregarious instinct of birds and mammals does not differ essentially, as I see, from the same instinct in man, except that in man it is often for coöperation or mutual protection, while with the lower animals it seems purely social. Many birds flock in the fall and winter that live in pairs during

the summer. Crows, for instance, have their rook-
eries, where vast numbers congregate to pass the
winter nights, and they usually keep in bands or
loose flocks during the winter days. Apparently,
this clannishness in winter is for social cheer and
good-fellowship alone. As they roost in naked,
exposed treetops, they could not, it seems to me,
perceptibly shield one another from the cold; while
it is reasonable to think that the greater scarcity
of food at this season would naturally cause them
to scatter. But the centripetal force, so to speak, of
the social instinct, triumphs over all else. Many
species of our birds flock in the fall — the various
blackbirds, the cedar-birds, the goldfinches, the
siskins, the snowbirds, the tree and bank swallows,
to say nothing of the waterfowl — some to migrate
and some to pass the winter here. In similar conditions or similar stress of circumstances, human
beings would probably act in a similar way; we
should migrate in herds, or face some common
calamity in large aggregates.

Indeed, the social instinct seems radically the
same in all forms of animal life. The loneliness of
a domestic animal separated from the herd, the
homesickness of a dog or a horse when removed
to a strange place, do not seem to differ very much
from the feelings we experience under like circumstances. Attachment to places, attachment to persons, attachment to one another, to home and to

mate — these feelings seem about the same in kind among all creatures. Of course they are more complex, far-reaching, and abiding in man than in the animals below him, but their genesis seems the same.

Among both birds and four-footed beasts, the maternal affection is doubtless greater than the paternal, and this also is human. But how brief and fugitive the affection is, compared with the same attachment in our own species! — of a few weeks' duration among our common birds, and a few months or a year among the mammals, but always as long as the well-being of the young requires it. When they become self-supporting, the parental affection ceases. And in a limited sense this is true in our own case.

If a bird loses its mate during the breeding season, the period of mourning and waiting is very brief, usually not more than a day or two. The need of rearing a family is urgent, and nature wastes no time in unavailing regrets. Just how the bereaved mate makes her or his wants known, I never could find out; but it seems there are always not far off some unmated birds of both sexes that are ready to step in and complete the circle once more. From sparrows to eagles, this seems to be the rule.

With what species, if any, the marriage unions last during life, I do not know. Neither do I know if anything like divorce, or unfaithfulness, or free love, ever takes place among the monogamous birds — probably not. The riot of the breeding instinct in the males confines itself to gay plumes, or songs, or grotesque antics, while the seriousness and preoccupation of the female, I doubt not, would prove an effectual warning to any gay Lothario among her neighbors, if such there happened to be.

I am convinced that birds have a sense of home, or something analogous to it, and that they return year after year to the same localities to nest. The few cases where I have been able to identify the particular sparrow or robin or bluebird confirm me in this belief.

Hermits among the birds or beasts are probably very rare, and I doubt if voluntary seclusion ever occurs. Sometimes an old male, vanquished and in a measure disabled by his younger rivals, may be driven out of the herd or pack and compelled to spend the remainder of his days in comparative solitude. Or an old eagle that has lost its mate may spend its days henceforth alone. The birds of prey, like the animals of prey, and like prowlers and bloodsuckers generally, are solitary in their habits.

The feeling of hostility towards strangers that all animals manifest in varying degrees, how distinctly we can trace it up through the savage races and through the lower orders of our social aggre-

gates, till it quite fades out in the more highly civ-
ilized communities!

Animals experience grief over the loss of their
young, but not over the death of a member of
their flock or tribe. Death itself seems to have no
meaning to them. When a bird seems to mourn
for its lost mate, its act is probably the outcry of
the breeding instinct which has been thwarted.

Do the birds and mammals sympathize with one
another? When one bird utters a cry of distress, the
birds of other species within hearing will hasten
to the spot and join in the cry — at least in the
breeding season. I have no proof that they will do
it at other times. And I do not call this sympathy,
but simply the alarm of the parental instinct, which
at this season is very sensitive. The alarm-cry of
many birds will often put four-footed animals on
the lookout. The language of distress and alarm
is a universal language, which all creatures understand more or less. But I doubt if sympathy as we
know it — the keen appreciation of the suffering
or the misfortune of another, which implies power
in a measure to put ourselves in that other's place
— even in its rudimentary form, exists among the
lower orders. Among the domestic fowls, a cry of
distress from one of them usually alarms the others:
a cry from a chicken brings the mother hen to the
rescue; this is the maternal instinct, and the instinct
of self-preservation which all animals must have or

their race would perish. A certain agonized call from a member of a herd of cattle will at once bring the other members to the spot, with uplifted heads and threatening horns. This, again, is the instinct of self-preservation. This, I say, animals must have, but they do not have to have sympathy any more than they have to have veneration, or humility, or the æsthetic sense. But fear — think how important this is to them — blind, unreasoning fear, but always alert and suspicious.

Fear in the human species is undoubtedly of animal origin. How acute it often is in young children — the fear of the dark, of the big, of the strange, and of the unusual! The first fear I myself remember was that of an open door at night leading into a dark room. What a horror I felt at that mysterious cavernous darkness! — and this without any idea of the danger that might lurk there. The next fear I recall was a kind of panic, when I was probably three or four years of age, at the sight of a hen-hawk sailing against the sky above me. I hurriedly climbed over the wall and hid behind it. Later, when I was ten or twelve years of age, my fear took a less animal form — a fear of spooks and hobgoblins, induced, no doubt, by the fearsome superstitions of my elders. Now I am not conscious of any physical or superstitious fears, but there is plenty of moral cowardice left. My little granddaughter, when two and a half years old, was filled with terror of the sea as she saw it for the first time from the beach.

Fear seems to have the same effect upon both man and beast, causing trembling of the muscles, a rapid beating of the heart, a relaxation of the sphincters, momentary weakness, confusion, panic, flight. It would be interesting to know if the blood leaves the capillaries in the faces of animals during sudden fright, as it does in man, producing paleness.

The panic that sometimes seizes a multitude of animals, resulting in a stampede, a blind, furious rush away from the real or the imaginary danger, seems to differ but little from that which at times seizes the human multitude in theatre, or circus, or on the field of battle. It is a kind of madness, augmented and intensified by numbers. The contagion of fear works among all creatures, like the contagion of joy, or anger, or any other sudden impulse. These things are " catching;" an emotional state in one man or one animal tends to beget the same state in all other near-by men or animals, either through imitation, or through some psychic law not well understood. Like begets like throughout nature. Just as our bodily temperature rises in a crowd, so does that psychic state become more acute in which we are liable to sudden enthusiasms or panic, fear or animal cruelty. Mobs are guilty of things, especially in the way of violence, that the separate members of them would never think of doing, just as nations and corporations will exhibit a meanness and hoggishness that would shame the individuals composing them.

It is a question whether or not the lower animals ever experience the feeling we know as revenge — that they cherish a hatred or a secret enmity toward one of their own kind or toward a person, in the absence of that person or fellow. Their power of association, which is undoubted, would call up the old anger on the sight of an object that had injured them, but they probably do not in the meantime carry any feeling of ill-will as we do, because they do not form mental concepts. And yet I have known things to happen that point that way. It is well known that the blue jay destroys the eggs of other birds. One day I found a nest of a blue jay with its five eggs freshly punctured — each egg with a small hole in it as if made by the beak of a small bird, as it doubtless had been. Was this revenge on the part of some victim of the jay's? One can only conjecture. Roosevelt tells this curiously human anecdote of a bear. A female grizzly was found by a hunter lying across a game trail in the woods. The hunter shot the bear as she was about to charge him, and on examining the spot where she had been lying, he found that it was the freshly made grave of her cub. He conjectured that a male grizzly or a cougar had killed the cub in the absence of the mother, and that on her return she had buried it, and had lain down upon the grave waiting to wreak her vengeance upon the murderer of her young. But this may be only the plausible human interpretation of the fact. Just what the bear's state of mind was, we have no means of knowing.

The dog undoubtedly exhibits more human traits than any other lower animal, and this by reason of his long association with man. There are few of our ordinary emotions that the dog does not share, as joy, fun, love of adventure, jealousy, suspicion, comradeship, helpfulness, guilt, covetousness, and the like, or feelings analogous to these — the dog version of them. I am not sure but that the dog is capable of contempt. The behavior at times of a large dog toward a small, the slights he will put upon him, even ejecting his urine upon him, is hardly capable of any other interpretation. The forbearance, too, which a large dog usually shows toward a touchy little whiffet, never resenting its impudent attacks, is very human. "A barking dog never bites" is an old saying founded upon human nature as well as upon dog nature. The noisy blusterer is rarely dangerous, whether man or dog. I do not agree with Stevenson that the dog is a snob. The key to a dog's heart is kindness. He will always meet you halfway and more. I have been asked why the farm dog usually shows such hostility to tramps and all disreputable-looking persons. It is not their looks that disturb the dog, but

143

their smell — a strange, unknown odor. This at once puts him on his guard and excites his enmity. There is little speculation in the eye of a dog, but his nose is keen and analytical.

The dog, through his long intercourse with man, has become charged with our human quality, as steel is charged by a magnet. Yet I am told that a tame wolf or a tame fox fawns and wags his tail and tries to lick his master's face, the same as the dog. At any rate, the dog does many things that we can name only in terms applicable to ourselves. My dog coaxes me to go for a walk, he coaxes me to get upon my lap, he coaxes for the food I am eating. When I upbraid him, he looks repentant and humiliated. When I whip him, he cries, when I praise him, he bounds, when I greet him in the morning, he whines with joy. It is not the words that count with him, it is the tone of the voice.

When I start out for a walk, he waits and dances about till he sees which way I am going. It seems as if he must at such times have some sort of mental process similar to my own under like circumstances. Or is his whole behavior automatic — his attitude of eagerness, expectancy, inquiry, and all? as automatic as the wagging of his tail when he is pleased, or as his bristling up when he is angry? It evinces some sort of mental action, but the nature of it is hard to divine. When he sits looking vaguely out upon the landscape, or rests his chin upon his paws and gazes into the fire, I wish I knew if there were anything like currents of thought, or reminiscences, or anticipations passing through his mind. When I speak sternly to him and he cowers down or throws himself on his back and puts up his paws pleadingly, I wish I knew just the state of his mind then. One day my dog deserted me while I was hunting, and when I returned, and before I had spoken a word to him, he came creeping up to me in the most abject way, threw himself over, and put up his pleading paws, as if begging forgiveness. Was he? We should call it that in a person. Yet I remember that I upbraided him when he first showed the inclination to desert me, and that fact may account for his subsequent behavior.

When you speak to your dog in a certain way, why does he come up to you and put out his front legs and stretch, and then stretch his hind legs, and maybe open his mouth and gape? Is it an affectation, or a little embarrassment because he does not know what you are saying? All dogs do it. The human traits of the dog are very obvious. One time I drove many miles through the country with my small mongrel black and tan dog Lark with me, often on the seat by my side. When he was in the wagon and other dogs came out and barked at us, Lark was very brave and answered back defiantly and threateningly; but when he was upon the ground and other dogs came out, Lark was as meek and non-resisting as a Quaker. Then let me take him up out of harm's way, and see how his tone would change, and what a setting-out he would give those dogs!

I do not believe that animals ever commit suicide. I do not believe that they have any notions of death, or take any note of time, or ever put up any " bluff game," or ever deliberate together, or form plans, or forecast the seasons. They may practice deception, as when a bird feigns lameness or paralysis to decoy you away from her nest, but this of course is instinctive and not conscious deception. There is on occasion something that suggests coöperation among them, as when wolves hunt in relays, as they are said to do, or when they hunt in couples, one engaging the quarry in front, while the other assaults it from the rear; or when quail roost upon the ground in a ring, their tails to the centre, their heads outward; or when cattle or horses form a circle when attacked in the open by wild beasts, the cattle with their heads outward, and the horses with their heels. Of course all this is instinctive, and not the result of deliberation. The horse always turns his tail to the storm as well, and cows and steers, if I remember rightly, turn their heads.

A family of beavers work together in building their dam, but whether or not they combine their strength upon any one object and thus achieve unitedly what they could not singly, I do not know.

Of course among the bees there is coöperation and division of labor, but how much conscious intelligence enters into the matter is beyond finding out.

Leadership among the animals, when it occurs, as among savage tribes, usually falls to the strong, to the most capable. And such leaders are self-elected: there is nothing like a democracy in the animal world. Troops of wild horses are said always to have a leader, and it is probable that bands of elk and reindeer do also. Flocks of migrating geese and swans are supposed to be led by the strongest old males; but among our flocking small birds I have never been able to discover anything like leadership. The whole flock acts as a unit, and performs its astonishing evolutions without leaders or signals.

In my youth, upon the farm, I observed that in a dairy of cows there was always one master cow, one to whose authoritative sniff, or gesture, or thrust, all others yielded, and she was usually the most quiet and peaceful cow in the herd.

The male animal, as compared with the female, is usually the more aggressive and domineering, except among birds of prey, where the reverse is true. Roosevelt says that a band of antelope, as of elk and deer, is ordinarily led by an old doe, but that when danger threatens, a buck may spring to the leadership.

In the breeding season the pronghorn buck has

his harems — all the does he can steal or cajole or capture from his rivals. "I have seen a comparatively young buck," says Roosevelt, "who had appropriated a doe, hustle her hastily out of the country as soon as he saw another antelope in the neighborhood; while on the other hand, a big buck, already with a good herd of does, will do his best to appropriate any other that comes in sight."

On the seal islands of Alaska we saw many old bull seals with their harems about them — a dozen or more demure-looking females resting upon low bowlders, while their lord and master sat perched above them on a higher rock. The defeated males, too young or too old to hold their own against their rivals, hung in ill-humored dejection about the neighborhood. I have read that on the Pampas in South America, wild stallions will capture and hurry away domestic mares, if they have a chance.

Animals are undoubtedly capable of feeling what we call worry and anxiety just as distinctly as they feel alarm or joy, only, of course, these emotions are much more complex in man. How the mother bird seems to worry as you near her nest or her young; how uneasy the cow is when separated from her calf, or the dog when he has lost his master! Do these dumb kindred of ours experience doubts and longings and suspicions and disappointments and hopes deferred just as we do? — the same in kind, if not in degree?

HUMAN TRAITS IN THE ANIMALS

The sheer agony or terror which an animal is capable of feeling always excites our pity. Roosevelt tells of once coming upon a deer in snow so deep that its efforts to flee were fruitless. As he came alongside of it, of course to pass it by untouched, it fell over on its side and bleated in terror. When John Muir and his dog Stickeen, at the imminent peril of their lives, at last got over that terrible crevasse in the Alaska glacier, the dog's demonstrations of joy were very touching. He raced and bounded and cut capers and barked and felicitated himself and his master as only a dog can.

The play of animals seems strictly analogous to the play of man, and I have no doubt that the reason of the one, whatever that be, is the reason of the other. Whether play is to be accounted for upon the theory of surplus energy, as Spencer maintains, or upon the theory of instinctive training and development — a sort of natural, spontaneous school or kindergarten that has reference to the future wants of the animal, as the German psychologist Karl Groos argues — a biological conception of play — its genesis is no doubt the same both in man and beast. The main difference is that the play of one is aimless and haphazard, while that of the other has method and purpose. Animals have no rules or systems, and yet I have often seen two red squirrels engaged in what seemed precisely analogous to the boys' game of tag. Up and down and

149

from tree to tree they would go, until one of them overtook the other, when it seemed to become its turn to flee and be pursued. But just how much method there is in such a game, it is impossible to determine. In all cases, the play of animals tends to develop those powers of speed, or agility, or strength that their ways of living call for. The spirit of play gradually leaves an animal at maturity, as it leaves man.

A trait alike common to man and beast is imitativeness; both are naturally inclined to do what they see their fellows do. The younger children imitate the elder, the elder imitate their parents, their parents imitate their neighbors. The young writer imitates the old, the young artist copies the master. We catch the trick of speech or the accent of those we much associate with; we probably, in a measure, even catch their looks. Any fashion of dress or equipage is as catching as the measles. We are more or less copyists all our lives. Among the animals, the young do what they see their parents do; this, I am convinced, is all there is of parental instruction among them; the young unconsciously follow the example of their elders. The bird learns the song of its parent. If it never hears this song, it may develop a song of its own — like its parent's song in quality, of course, but unlike it in form. Or it may acquire the song of some other species.

HUMAN TRAITS IN THE ANIMALS

Darwin thinks that birds have "nearly the same taste for the beautiful as we have," except, of course, that in man "the sense of beauty is manifestly a more complex feeling and is associated with various intellectual ideas." It seems to me that if we mean by taste the appreciation of the beautiful, it is as distinctly a human gift as reason is, or as is the sense of humor, or the perception of the spiritual and the ideal. Shall we say the lilies of the field have taste because Solomon in all his glory was not arrayed like one of these? or that the trees have taste because of their grace and beauty of form? or the insects because of their many beautiful colors and patterns? I doubt if the æsthetic feeling is even rudimentary in birds, any more than are our moral and other intellectual traits. It is thought that the male bird sings to charm the female. Are such discordant notes, then, as the gobble of the turkey, the crowing of the cock, the scream of the peacock or of the guinea hen, to charm the female? When the rooster crows, the nearby hens shake their heads as if the sound pained them, as doubtless it does.

Why, then, do birds sing? Is it from a love of beautiful sounds? I can only answer that it seems to be a trait inherent in the male sexual principle, as much so as are gay plumes and ornamental appendages; it is one of the secondary sexual characteristics. It is very significant that the sweetest songsters to our ears are, as a rule, of the plainest colors and free from extra plumes and ornaments. I have yet to discover any evidence of pleasure on the part of the female in the songs of her male suitors. The male does not even sing for his own ear; if he did, when his vocal powers are defective, as is sometimes the case, he would quit singing. But such is not the case; he sings because he has the impulse to sing, and that is reason enough.

I know but one fact in the life of our birds that suggests anything like taste. I refer to the nesting-habits of the hummingbird, and of the little blue-gray gnatcatcher and the wood pewee. The nests of these birds are always neatly thatched with lichens, thus perfectly realizing the dream of the true domestic architect, of making the structure blend with its surroundings. The nests of nearly all birds blend well with their surroundings, because the material at hand is itself of a dull, neutral character. But the lichens which the hummer and the gnatcatcher and our wood pewee use seem, at first sight, an extra touch. Yet I cannot credit it to taste or to the love of the beautiful, because it is beautiful only to the cultivated, artistic taste of man. To a savage, or even to those much higher in civilization, it would not appear beautiful. A certain degree of culture has to be reached before we find beauty in these quieter things. The reason why these birds thatch the outside of their nests with lichens is doubtless this : the nests are built of a kind of down that would render them very frail and pervious to the rain were they not stayed and thatched with some firmer material. The lichens and spiders' webs bind them together and keep them in shape. Hence I should say that utility alone governed the bird in this use of lichens. Bright objects attract children, attract birds, attract quadrupeds, but this attraction is far enough from what we mean by taste or the love of the beautiful.

VIII

ANIMAL AND PLANT INTELLIGENCE

I

WHEN I hear a person expatiating on the reasoning powers of the lower animals, as I very often do, I want to tell him of the wonderful reasoning powers of the flies that pester our cow in summer. Those flies have measured the length of the old cow's tail so accurately that they know the precise spot on her body where the tail cannot reach them; on these spots they settle and torment her. Their behavior reveals great powers of calculation and reasoning. By what means they measured the swing of that tail so accurately I do not know. When I come slying up with a switch in my hand, they dart away before I can get in a stroke, because they know I can reach them; they take the measure of my arm and switch on the instant — on the fly, as it were. And what shall we say of the mosquito that so quickly finds out the vulnerable parts of one's clothing? If one chances to be wearing low shoes, does she not know at a glance where to strike, though she may never have seen low shoes before?

Now is not that reasoning just as good as much of the reasoning that the public indulges in upon these subjects? Or, take the wit of the old cow herself. Yonder is a very steep hillside, the high, abrupt bank of an old river terrace. Along this bank the cattle have made a series of parallel paths, level as the top of the terrace itself. The paths, I should think, are about four feet apart, just far enough so that the cow walking along one of them can graze at her ease over all the strip of ground that lies between it and the next path. When she comes to the end, she steps up into the path above and repeats the process, and so on till the whole side of the terrace has been grazed over. Does not this show that the cow is very level-headed, that she can meet a difficult problem and solve it as rationally as you or I? Without the paths, how awkward and difficult the grazing would be! Now it is done easily because it is done from level paths; it is done thoroughly because it is done systematically. If you or I were going to search that hillside over daily, should not we adopt similar or identical tactics?

In Idaho I saw that the grazing sheep had terraced the grassy mountain-sides in the same way. Their level paths were visible from afar. How inevitable and free from calculation it all is! The grazing cattle take the easiest way, and this way is horizontally along the face of the hill. To take the hill by a straight climb or diagonally would be labor, so the animal moves easily along its side, cropping the grass within reach. Then she takes a step or two upward and grazes back the other way, and this process is repeated till a series of level parallel paths are worn in the side of the hill. They are as much a natural result as is the river terrace itself.

The cow has always been a famous engineer in laying out paths; sheep are, too. They take the line of least resistance; they ford the streams at the best places; they cross the mountains in the deep notches; they scale the hills by the easiest grade. Shall we, therefore, credit them with reason?

When I was a bucolic treasury clerk in Washington, the cow of an old Irishwoman near by used to peep through the cracks in my garden fence at my growing corn and cabbage till her mouth watered. Then she saw that a place in the fence yielded to me and let me in, so she tried it; she nudged the gate with her nose until she hit the latch, and the gate swung open by its own weight and let her in. There was an audible crunching of succulent leaves and stalks that soon attracted my attention. I hustled her out, and sent a kick after her that fell short and nearly unjointed my leg. But she was soon back, and she came again and again till I discovered her secret and repaired the latch so that nudging or butting the gate would not open it. How surely such conduct as this of the cow's evinces reason to most persons! But shall we not rather call it the blind gropings of instinct stimulated into action by the sight and odor of the tender vegetables? Many of the lowest organisms show just as much intelligence about their food as did the old cow. Even the American sundew, according to Mrs. Treat, will move its leaves so that it can seize a fly pinned half an inch from it. The method of the old cow was that of hit and miss, or trial and error. She wanted the corn, and she butted the gate, and as luck would have it, when she hit the latch the gate swung open. But shall we conclude that the beast had any idea of the principle of the gate? Or any idea at all but the sense impression made upon her hunger by the growing vegetables? Animals do not connect cause and effect as we do by thinking the "therefore;" they simply associate one thing with another. Your dog learns to associate your act of taking your hat and cane with a walk, or your gun with the delights of the chase, or with its report, if he is afraid of it, and so on. Without this power of association the birds and beasts could not get on in life; the continuity of their experience would be broken. It is a rude kind of memory — sense memory. A sense impression to-day revives a sense impression of yesterday, or of the day before, and that is about all there is of it.

ANIMAL AND PLANT INTELLIGENCE

While I am telling tales on old Brindle, let me mention another point. Most farmers and country people think that the "giving down" or "holding up" of the milk by the cow is a voluntary act. In fact, they fancy that the udder is a vessel filled with milk, and that the cow releases it or withholds it just as she chooses. But the udder is a manufactory; it is filled with blood, from which the milk is manufactured while you milk. This process is controlled by the cow's nervous system. When she is excited or in any way disturbed, as by a stranger, or by the taking away of her calf, or any other cause, the process is arrested and the milk will not flow. The nervous energy goes elsewhere. The whole process is as involuntary as is digestion in man, and is disturbed or arrested in about the same way.

Why should we not credit the child with reason when it is learning to walk, and with a knowledge of the law of gravity? See how carefully it poises itself on the feet and adjusts itself to the pull of the invisible force. It is a natural philosopher from the cradle, and knows all about the necessity of keeping the centre of gravity within the base if it would avoid a fall! But there is probably less calculation in all this than there appears to be, since Huxley tells us that a frog with most of its brain removed will keep its position on the top of the hand while you slowly turn it over. It, too, feels the pull of gravity and knows all about the importance of keeping the centre within the base. Throw this brainless frog into the water, and it swims as well as ever it did. Dan Beard, in his delightful "Animal Book," says that a rattlesnake which had just had its head cut off, coiled and struck him with the bloody stump when he touched it as promptly as it would have done with its head on. So it is doubtless true that all creatures do many reasonable and natural things without possessing the faculty of reason. Much of our own conduct in life is the result of this same unconscious, unreasoning obedience to natural forces or innate tendencies.

The English psychologist Hobhouse gives an account, in his work on "Mind and Evolution," of the experiments he tried with cats, dogs, monkeys, an otter, and an elephant, to test their intelligence. Their food was placed in boxes or jars, or tied to a string, in such ways that to get at it the animal had to do certain definite concrete things that it could not have been called upon to do in the ordinary course of its natural life, such as pulling strings, working levers, drawing bolts, lifting latches, opening drawers, upsetting jugs, always stimulated by the prospect of food. After many trials at the various tricks, a little gleam of intelligence seemed to pass through their minds. It was as if a man without power to move should finally feebly lift a hand or shake his head. The elephant was taught to pull a bolt and open the lid of a box only by her keeper taking her trunk in his hand and guiding it through each movement, stage by stage. She learned to pull the bolt on the seventh trial, but could not learn the three movements of drawing bolt, opening lid, and holding it open, till the fortieth trial, on the third day. Sometimes she tried to lift the lid before she drew the bolt, sometimes she pushed the bolt the wrong way. Another elephant learned to draw the bolt on the fourth trial. The otter learned to draw the bolt after seeing it drawn twelve times. Jack, the dog, learned to do the trick in his pawing, blundering way after many trials. A bolt furnished with a knob so that it could not be drawn all the way out worried all the animals a good deal. The dog had ninety lessons, and yet did not clearly understand the trick. The monkeys and the chimpanzee learned the different tricks more readily than the other animals, but there "appeared to be no essential difference in capacity to learn between the dogs, the elephants, the cats, and others." None of the animals seemed to appreciate the point of the trick, the dependence of one thing upon another, or the *why* of any particular movement. Poor things! their strenuous intellectual efforts in drawing a bolt or working a lever used to tire them very much. Sometimes, under the tutelage of their trainers, they would seem to show a gleam of real intelligence, as when you fan a dull ember till it glows a little. The next hour or the next day the ember had lost its glow and had to be fanned again. Yet they all did improve in doing their little "stunts," but how much was awakened intelligence, and how much mere force of habit, one could not be quite sure.

Hobhouse is no doubt right when he says that intelligence arises within the sphere of instinct, and that the former often modifies the action of the latter. The extent to which the lower animals profit by experience is a measure of their intelligence. If they hit upon new and improved ways spontaneously, or adapt new means to an end, they show a measure of intelligence. I once stopped up the entrance to a black hornets' nest with cotton. The hornets removed the cotton by chewing off the fibres that held it to the nest, and then proceeded to change the entrance by carrying it farther around toward the wall of the house, so that the feat of stopping it up was not so easy. Was this an act of intelligence, or only an evidence of the plasticity or resourcefulness of instinct? But if a dog in stalking a woodchuck (and I have been told of such things) at the critical moment were to rush to the woodchuck's hole so as to get there before it, this were an act of intelligence. To hunt and stalk is instinctive in the dog, but to correlate its act to that of its prey in this manner would show the triumph of intelligence over instinct.

ANIMAL AND PLANT INTELLIGENCE

II

Huxley thought that because of the absence of language the brutes can have no trains of thought but only trains of feeling, and this is the opinion of most comparative psychologists. I am myself quite ready to admit that the lower animals come as near to reasoning as they come to having a language. Their various cries and calls — the call to the mate, to the young, the cry of anger, of fear, of alarm, of pain, of joy — do serve as the medium of some sort of communication, but they do not stand for ideas or mental concepts any more than the various cries of a child do. They are the result of simple reactions to outward objects or to inward wants, and do not imply any mental process whatever. A grown person may utter a cry of pain or fear or pleasure with a mind utterly blank of any ideas. Once on a moonlight night I lay in wait for some boy poachers in my vineyard. As I suddenly rose up, clad in a long black cloak, and rushed for one and seized his leg as he was hastening over the fence, he uttered a wild, agonized scream precisely as a wild animal does when suddenly seized. He told me afterward that he was fairly frightened out of his wits. For the moment he was simply an unreasoning animal.

A language has to be learned, but the animals all use their various calls and cries instinctively.

What a clear case is that of the hen when she brings off her first brood! She speaks a language which she never spoke before, and her chickens hear a language which they never heard before, and understand it instantly. When the mother hen calls them, they come; when she utters her alarm-note, they hide, or run to her for protection.

The various calls and cries of the animals have just about the same significance as do their gestures of bristling, arching, pawing, and so on. They are understood by their fellows, and they are expressive of emotions and not of ideas. The loud cackling of a rooster which I hear as I write expresses in a vague way some excitement, pleasurable or otherwise. Or he may be signaling to the cackling hen to guide her to the flock, an instinct inherited from his jungle-fowl ancestors.

The parrot, of course, does not know the meaning of the words it repeats so glibly; it only associates certain sounds with certain acts or occasions, and says "Good-by," or "Come in," at the right time because it has been taught to connect these sounds with certain sense impressions through the eye and ear. When a child is in pain, it cries; when it is pleased, it laughs: always are its various sounds expressive of some immediate concrete want or experience. This is the character of all animal language; it does not express ideas, but feelings — emotions then and there experienced —

the result of an inward impulse or an outward condition.

With ourselves, emotion arises spontaneously and is not the result of will. We cannot be angry, or joyous, or depressed, or experience the emotion of the beautiful, or of the sublime, or of love, or terror, by mere willing. These emotions arise under certain conditions that are not matters of will or calculation. If a man does not flee from danger, real or imaginary, like an animal, it is because his reason or his pride has stepped in and stopped him. Man's reason shows itself in checking or controlling his emotion, while the lower animals have no such check or stay. A man may think about the danger from which he flees, or about the scene that thrilled him, or of the woman that moved him, but the thinking always follows the emotion, while the horse or the dog flees without stopping to think.

Without doubt, to me at least, man has climbed up from some lower animal form, but he has, as it were, pulled the ladder up after him. None of man's humbler kindred, even if man were to reach them a hand, or a dozen hands, could now mount to the human plane.

As there must be a point back along the line of our descent where consciousness began — consciousness in the animal and self-consciousness in man — so there must be a point where reason began. If we had all the missing links in the chain,

165

no doubt we might, approximately at least, determine the form in which it first dawned. The higher anthropoid apes, which are, probably, a lateral branch of the stem of the great biological tree that bore man, show occasional gleams of it, but reason, as we ascribe it to the lower orders, is more a kind of symptomatic reason, a vague foreshadowing of reason rather than the substance itself. For a long time the child is without reason, or any mental concepts, and all its activities are reactions to stimuli, like those of an animal; it is merely a bundle of instincts, but by and by it begins to show something higher and we hail the dawn of reason, and the child's development from the animal plane into the human.

The development of reason in the race of man has of course been as gradual as the development of his body from some lower animal form, but is it any more startling or miraculous than those slow transmutations or transformations which we trace everywhere in nature, and which in the end amount to complete metamorphosis? It is a new thing in the animal world, and separates man from the lower orders by an impassable gulf. The gulf has been crossed in the past; not by a sudden leap, but by slow growth and transmutation, just as the gulf between the bird and reptile, or between the reptile and the amphibian, has been crossed. Man is separated from the lower orders less by a physical than by a psychological gulf. His anatomy is fundamentally the same, though there is doubtless an invisible gulf in the molecules of the brain cells; but his psychology is fundamentally different. Is this difference any greater, it may be asked, than that which separates the highest human intelligence from that of the lowest savage? I look upon it more as a difference of kind than of degree. It is comparatively easy to trace a continuous line of development from the mind of the Hottentot to the mind of the foremost European, but between the savage and our pithecoid ancestors there are many missing links. The evolutionary process that must have connected them has worked out something like a metamorphosis.

Darwin in seeking to prove the animal origin of man felt called upon to show at least the rudiments of man's reasoning powers in his humbler beginnings. Certain it is that evolution must have something to go upon. But does it not have enough to go upon in the kind of intelligence the unthinking animal world exhibits? The slow metamorphosis of this into human reason is no more difficult to conceive of than a hundred other slow metamorphoses that may be traced in nature, wherein we see the adult animal totally unlike its youthful beginning, or where we see two chemical elements uniting to form a third entirely unlike either. Animal and vegetable life doubtless had a common origin, but behold how they have diverged. How could the intelligence of one have been evolved out of the intelligence of the other without this mystery of slow metamorphosis?

I do not know how far back along the line of evolution in animal life biologists place the beginning of the sense of sight, certainly the highest of all bodily senses. But it must have begun somewhere a good way this side of the first unicellular life; the eye as an organ and as we know it is doubtless a late development. And what a marvel it is! What can be a greater departure from the sense of touch and taste and smell — more like a miraculous addition or metamorphosis — than the sense of sight? And yet its foundation is the same as that of the other senses, nerve sensibility.

Or take another near-at-hand illustration. What can seem more like a new birth, a new creation, than the flower of a plant when contrasted with its leaves and stalk and root? Yet all this delicacy and color and fragrance come by way of these humbler parts; indeed, lay dormant there in the soil till this something we call life drew them out of it and built them up into this exquisite form. In the same way, may not the animal nature in the course of long ages have blossomed into the mental and spiritual powers which man possesses, and which are only latent in the lower creatures? We see the miracle of the flower daily, but the other miracle is a slow process that no man has witnessed or can witness. Strike out the element of time, and we see it as we see the stalk bring forth the flower, or as we see the grub metamorphosed into the butterfly.

We turn smoke into flame by supplying the fire with a little more oxygen. Has any new thing been added? What is added to transmute animal intelligence into human seems to be only more oxygen — more of that which favors mental combustion — more brain matter and a finer nervous organization.

III

We translate the action of bird and beast into human thought just as we translate their cries and calls into human speech. But the bird does not utter the words we ascribe to it, it only makes a sound that suggests the words. So its behavior is not the result of thought, but it is such as to suggest thought to a thinking animal, and we proceed to explain it in terms of thought.

We see a crow approaching a bit of meat upon the lawn in winter and note his suspicion. He circles about and surveys it from all points and approaches it with extreme caution, and we say he suspects some trap or concealed enemy, or plot to do him injury, when in fact he does not consciously suspect anything or think anything; he is simply obeying his inborn instinct to be on the lookout for danger at all times and in all places — the instinct

169

of self-preservation. When the chickadee comes to the bone or bit of suet upon the tree under your window, it does so with little or no signs of suspicion. Its enemies are of a different kind, and its instincts work differently. Or when we see a fox trying to elude or delay the hound that is pursuing him, by taking to rail fences or bare plowed fields, or to the ice of frozen streams, we say he knows what he is doing; he knows his scent will not lie upon the rail or the bare earth or the ice as upon the snow or the moist ground. We translate his act into our mental concepts. The fox is, of course, trying to elude or to shake off his pursuer, but he is not drawing upon his stores of natural knowledge or his powers of thought to do so; he does not realize as you or I would that it is the scent of his foot that gives the clue to his enemy. How can he have any general ideas about odors and surfaces that best retain them? He is simply obeying the instinctive cunning of his vulpine nature, and takes to the fence or to the ice or to the water as a new expedient when others have failed. Such a course on our part under like circumstances would be the result of some sort of mental process, but with the fox it is evidence of the flexibility and resourcefulness of instinct. The animals all do rational things without reason, cunning things without calculation, and provident things without forethought. Of course we have to fall back upon instinct to account for their acts — that natural " propensity," as Paley defined it, which is " prior to experience and independent of instruction."

In both the animal and vegetable worlds we see a kind of intelligence that we are always tempted to describe in terms of our own intelligence; it seems to run parallel to and to foreshadow our own as to ways and means and getting on in the world — propagation, preservation, dissemination, adaptation — the plant resorting to many ingenious devices to scatter its seed and to secure cross-fertilization; the animal eluding its enemies, hiding its door or its nest, finding its way, securing its food, and many other things — all exhibiting a kind of intelligence that is independent of instruction or experience, and that suggests human reason without being one with it. Each knows what its kind knows, and each does what its kind does, but only in man do we reach self-knowledge and the freedom of conscious intelligence.

The animals all profit more or less by experience, and this would at first thought seem to imply some sort of mental capacity. But vegetables profit by experience also, and mainly in the same way, by increasing power to live and multiply. Hunt an animal and it becomes wary and hardy; persecute a plant and it, too, seems to tighten its hold upon life. How hardy and prolific are the weeds against which every man's hand is turned! How full of resources they are; how they manage to shift for themselves, while the cultivated plants are tender and helpless in comparison! Pull up redroot in your garden and lay it on the ground, and the chances are that one or more rootlets that come in contact with the soil will take hold again and enable the plant to mature part of its seeds. This adaptability and tenacity of life is, no doubt, the result of the warfare waged against this weed by long generations of gardeners. Natural selection steps in and preserves the most hardy. Of course the individual animal profits more by experience than the individual plant, yet the individual plant profits also. Do not repeated transplantings make a plant more hardy and increase its chances of surviving? If it does not learn something, it acquires new powers, it profits by adversity.

IV

But as the animal is nearer to us than the vegetable, so is animal intelligence nearer akin to our own than plant intelligence. We hear of plant physiology, but not yet of plant psychology. When a plant growing in a darkened room leans toward the light, the leaning, we are taught, is a purely mechanical process, the effect of the light upon the cells of the plant brings it about in a purely mechanical way; but when an animal is drawn to the light, the process is a much more complex one, and implies a nervous system. It is thought by some that the roots of a water-loving plant divine the water from afar and run toward it. The truth is, the plant or tree sends its roots in all directions, but those on the side of the water find the ground moister in that direction and their growth is accelerated, while the others are checked by the dryness of the soil. An ash tree stood on a rocky slope where the soil is thin and poor, twenty or twenty-five feet from my garden. After a while it sent so many roots down into the garden, and so robbed the garden vegetables of the fertilizers, that we cut the roots off and dug a trench to keep the tree from sending more. Now the gardener thought the tree divined the rich pasturage down below there and reached for it accordingly. The truth is, I suppose, that the roots on that side found a little more and better soil, and so pushed on till they reached the garden, where they were at once so well fed that they multiplied and extended themselves rapidly. Both plant and tree know a good thing when they find it. How could they continue if they did not?

A birch tree starting life upon the top of a rock, — as birch trees more than any others are wont to do, — where the soil is thin, soon starts a root down to the ground several feet below in what seems a very intelligent way. Now the tree cannot know that the ground is there within reach. On one side of the rock, usually on the north side, it finds moss and moisture, and here the root makes its way. When it reaches the edge of the rocks, it bends down just as a fluid would do and continues its course till it reaches the ground; then it rejoices, so to speak. All other roots are called in or dry up, this one root increases till it is like a continuation of the trunk itself, and a new root system is established in the ground. But why we find the birch more often established upon a rock than any other tree, I do not yet know.

I know of a little birch tree that is planted in the niche on the face of an almost perpendicular rock in the edge of the woods. There has been a tree, probably a birch, in the same niche before it, and in this mould of its ancestor the tree is planted. It has wedged its roots into the rock wherever there is a seam or crack, and it must have thriven fairly well on its scant rations of soil for several years, or until it became a sapling the size of one's wrist. Then it started a root diagonally down the face of the rock toward the ground, about four feet distant. How that root made its way there on that bare, smooth surface, where there is only a thin wash of lichens, is a mystery. But it did, and it reached the ground and is now the size of a broom handle, and is doubtless the tree's main source of sustenance.

What prompted the tree to send it down, to organize and equip this relief expedition to the soil across the desert face of the rock? I have always supposed a growing root lived off the country it traveled over, but in this case it must have been fed from the rear; the tree pushed it on even when it brought in no supplies. How interesting it would be to know how far this root would have traveled across that bare rock-face had the ground been many yards away! Have trees more wit than is dreamed of in our philosophy?

The intelligence of the plants and flowers of which Maeterlinck writes so delightfully is, of course, only a manifestation of the general intelligence that pervades all nature. Maeterlinck is usually sound upon his facts, however free and poetic he may be in the interpretation of them. The plants and flowers certainly do some wonderful things; they secure definite ends by definite means and devices, as much so as does man himself — witness the elaborate and ingenious mechanical contrivances by which the orchids secure cross-fertilization. Yet if we are to use terms strictly, we can hardly call it intelligence in the human sense, that is, the result of reflection on the part of the plant itself, any more than we can ascribe the general structure and economy of the plant, or of our own bodies, to an individual act of intelligence.

There are ten thousand curious and wonderful things in both the animal and vegetable worlds, and in the organic world as well, but it is only in a poetic and imaginative sense that we can speak of them as the result of intelligence on the part of the things themselves: we personify the things when we do so. The universe is pervaded with mind, or with something for which we have no other name. But it is not as an ingenious machine, say the modern printing-press, is pervaded with mind. The machine is a senseless tool in the hands of an external intelligence; in nature we see that the intelligence is within and is inseparable from it. The machine is the result of mind, but things in nature seem the organs of mind.

IX

THE REASONABLE BUT UNREASONING
ANIMALS

I

THERE is to me a perennial interest in this question of animal instinct *versus* intelligence, and I trust my readers will pardon me if I again take the question up. Ever since one of our leading weekly journals (last June) declared its belief that "animals are capable of reasoning from certain premises, and do possess and express, though in a rudimentary form, many of the moral and intellectual processes and sentiments of man," I have wanted to take another shot at the subject. I do not now recall that any one has before claimed that the lower animals possess many of the moral sentiments of man, though a goodly number of persons seem to have persuaded themselves that animals do reason. Even so competent a naturalist as Mr. Hornaday says that asking if animals reason is to him like asking if fishes swim. But I suspect that Mr. Hornaday is a better naturalist than he is a comparative psychologist, because all the eminent comparative psychologists, so far as I know them, have reached the conclusion that animals do not reason. That eminent German psychologist, Wundt, says that the entire intellectual life of animals can be accounted for on the simple law of association; and Lloyd Morgan, the greatest of living English comparative psychologists, in his discussion of the question, "Do animals reason?" concludes that they do not — they do "not perceive the *why* and think the *therefore*." He urges, very justly, I think, that "in no case is an animal's activity to be interpreted as the outcome of a higher psychic faculty if it can fairly be interpreted as the outcome of faculties which are lower in the psychological scale." That is to say, Why impute reason to an animal if its behavior can be explained on the theory of instinct?

Some of our later nature writers seek to cut out instinct entirely, and call it all reason. If we cut out instinct, then we have two kinds of reason to account for and our last state is worse than our first. The young dog that in the house takes a bone and goes through the motions of burying it on the kitchen floor, digging the hole, putting it in, covering it up, and pressing the imaginary soil down with his nose, does not show the same kind of intelligence that even a child of four does when she puts her dolly in its little bed and carefully tucks it up. The one act is rational, the other is irrational; one is the result of observation, the other is inherited memory.

REASONABLE BUT UNREASONING

There is much in a hasty view of animal life that looks like reason, because instinct is a kind of intelligence and it acts in a reasonable manner. But when we get something like an inside view of the mind of the lower orders, we see how fundamentally it differs from the human. And we get this view of it, not in the ordinary course of the animal's life, because the ordinary course of its life is appointed by its inherited instincts, but under exceptional conditions, when it encounters a new problem. Now, when a reasoning intelligence is confronted by a new problem, it recognizes it as such, and, having a fund of knowledge and experience to draw upon, it proceeds to deal with it accordingly. Not so the animal; it does not know the new problem when it sees it, and in its dealings with it acts much like a machine that was made to do some other work.

Let me group together here a number of instances from animal life, some of which I have given elsewhere in my writings, which show how much nearer the lower orders come to being mere automata than they come to being reasoning intelligences.

Take the case of the robin or bluebird that may often be seen in the spring, day after day, dashing itself madly against a window-pane, fighting its fancied rival there in its own reflected image, and never discovering that it is being fooled even after it has taken a peep into the empty room inside

179

through a broken pane; or the case of the red squirrel that carried nuts all one day and put them into the end of a drain pipe that ran down an embankment wall and opened on to a pavement below, where the nuts behaved much as the water did that the pipe was meant to carry — they dropped down and rolled away across the street pavement. Or the case of the beaver that cut down a tree four times because the tree was held by the branches of other trees at the top so that it could not fall, but only dropped at each cutting the distance of the piece cut off. What finally decided the beaver to desist, it would be interesting to know. Or take the case of Hamerton's cow that in affection for her calf licked its stuffed skin till it ripped open and the hay with which it was stuffed fell out, when the bereaved mother proceeded to eat the hay with the utmost matter-of-course air.

During some long-gone time in the history of the raccoon it seems to have been needful for it to wash its food. Maybe the habit was acquired when it lived more exclusively than it does now upon fresh-water mussels, which it dug out of the mud along inland streams and lakes. At any rate, the coon now always washes its food, whether it needs washing or not, and in muddy water as promptly as in clear, so that the Germans call the coon the *Waschbär*. Ernest Harold Baynes tells me that he has taken young coons before their eyes were open, and brought them up on milk, and that the first time he gave them solid food, one of them took it and ran to a pail of water which it had never before seen, thrust the food into it, washed it, and then ate it. When no water was within reach, he has seen the coon rub the food a moment in its paws and then drop it. Dallas Lore Sharp says that his tame coon would go through the motions of washing its food on the upturned bottom of its empty tub, and that it would try to wash its oysters in the straw on the floor of its cage. This habit, I say, doubtless had its origin in some past need or condition of the life of the race of coons, and it persists after that need is gone.

The story that is told of the brakeman upon a train of cars in Russia, who at each stop of the train went from wheel to wheel, as was once the custom in all countries, and hit it a sharp blow with a hammer, saying on being asked why he did it, " I do not know, sir, it is my orders," illustrates very well the unreasoning character of animal instinct. The animal has its orders, but it does not think or ask why.

At Bahia Blanca, in South America, Darwin saw a bird, the casarita, that builds its nest in holes which it drills in the banks of streams like our kingfisher. At one place where he was stopping, the walls around the house were built of hardened mud, and were bored through and through with holes by these birds in their attempts to form their nests. The mud wall attracted them as if it had been a natural earth bank, and in trying to reach the proper depth for their nests, six feet or more, they invariably came through and out on the other side. Still they kept on drilling. Says Darwin : —

"I do not doubt that each bird, as often as it came to daylight on the opposite side, was greatly surprised at the marvelous fact."

I do not suppose the bird really experienced any feeling of surprise at all, any more than the bluebird above referred to did, when it looked into the vacant room and did not see the object of its wrath. The feeling of surprise comes to beings that understand the relation of cause and effect, which evidently the lower animals do not. Had the casarita been capable of the feeling of surprise, it would have been capable of seeing its own mistake.

Our high-hole is at times guilty of the same folly. When he drums on the metal ventilator or the tin leader upon your house, he has found a new thing, but it suits his purpose to make a noise to attract the attention of the female rather better than the dry stub did. And when he excavates a limb or tree-trunk for his nest, he acts like a reasonable being; but when he drills a hole through the clapboards of an empty building, and, not finding that the interior is what he wants, drills again and again, or perforates over and over the covering of an ice-house and lets out the sawdust, as I have often known him to do, what does he act like then?

Such instances reveal as by a flash of light the nature of animal mentality — how blindly, how automatically, the beasts act. If a person ever behaved in that way, we should say he had lost his mind, that reason was dethroned. We should not merely say he was unreasonable, we should say he was insane.

In its ordinary course of life the animal behaves in a reasonable manner, its course of action follows regular lines. Its progenitors have followed the same lines for countless generations; habit has worn a groove. But when a new, unheard-of condition confronts them, then there is no groove and their activity takes these irrational forms. When the phœbe-bird covers her nest in the ledge with moss, she does a reasonable thing; she blends it with the rock in a way that is both good art and good strategy. Now, if this were the result of reason, when she comes to the porch and to newly hewn timbers she would leave the moss off, because here it betrays rather than conceals her nest. But she sticks to her moss wherever she goes.

The same curious blundering may be seen in the insect world. For instance, the trap-door spiders in California make their nests in moss-covered ground and cover the lids of the doors with green growing moss. An English naturalist, as reported by Jordan and Kellogg in their "Animal Life," removed the moss and the other assimilative material from the door and found that the spider always replaced it. Then he removed it again, and with it the moss and débris from the ground in a large circle about the nest. This, of course, left the door as well concealed as before because it made it one with its surroundings. Did the spider leave it so? Not a bit of it. She fetched more moss and bits of bark and sticks and covered it as before, which gave away her secret completely. If she had done otherwise, or had covered her door with soil so as to make it one with its environment, we should have had to credit her with a faculty higher than instinct.

While speaking of insects in connection with this subject of the automatic character of animal intelligence, I am reminded of the habit of one of the solitary wasps as described by Fabre. When the wasp brings an insect to its hole, it lays it down at the entrance and backs down into the hole, apparently to make some examination, then comes out and drags in its prey. Fabre watched his opportunity, and, when the wasp had disappeared in her den, removed her game a few inches away. The wasp came out, hunted for her bug, found it and drew it back to its former position, then dropped it and retreated into her den as before. Fabre again drew the insect away, and again the wasp came out and repeated her former behavior. Time after time this little scene was enacted; the wasp *must* go into her den and make her preliminary survey before dragging in her prey. That habit had become fixed and there could be no deviation from it, and yet the wasps in many ways seem so surprisingly intelligent!

Another bee upon which Fabre experimented builds a cell of masonry, fills it with honey, lays her egg in it, and then seals it up. When the bee was away, Fabre punctured the half-filled cell and let the honey flow out. When the bee returned, she appeared to be disturbed to find her honey gone; she examined the hole through which it had escaped curiously, but made no attempt to repair it, and continued to pour in the honey the same as before. After she had brought the usual quantity — the quantity her forbears had always brought — she laid her egg in the empty cell and sealed it up. The machine had done its work, and it could do nothing not down in the ancestral specifications.

Dan Beard tells of an ichneumon-fly that tried all one day to thrust its ovipositor into a nail-head in a board in his cabin, mistaking the dark spot which the nail-head made for a hole that led to the burrow of a certain wood-borer which is the host of the ichneumon. Beard thinks the fly desisted only when it had seriously dulled the point of its instrument. I am reminded of one of our well-known wild flowers, the erythronium or fawn lily, that will persist in a

185

certain habit, no matter how many times defeated. This plant forms a new bulb each spring by sending out a big tap-root, that bores down into the ground and plants the new bulb deeper and deeper each season till the required depth of six or eight inches is reached. When the ground is so hard that the pioneer root cannot penetrate it, it wanders in loops over the surface and forms the new bulb no deeper than the old one was, and keeps this habit up spring after spring, groping its way blindly about over the hard surface.

As further illustration of the automatic character of animal instinct, take the case of the migrating lemmings in Norway and Sweden. At times the country gets overstocked with these rodents, when vast numbers of them migrate down from the hills toward the sea, swimming the lakes and rivers in their way. This seems a reasonable course, and is very much what men would do under like circumstances; their instincts accord with reason. But mark what follows: when the lemmings reach the sea, they plunge in and swim till they perish. Having got in motion, they go on, like any other natural force, till they have spent themselves. It is said that steamships have at times encountered these bands of swimming rodents and been half an hour in steaming through them. I do not suppose they mistake the sea for another lake or river such as they have already crossed; I do not suppose any notions or comparisons exist in their minds about it. An impulse to migrate, which is like a decree of nature, has taken possession of them, and they obey it blindly, to their own destruction. These incidents, which recur at intervals, afford another illustration of how radically animal instinct differs from human reason. It is a kind of fate.

Instinct may be thwarted in its efforts, but it cannot be convinced that its effort is wrong, or has failed. One spring, as I have elsewhere related, a pair of English sparrows, in searching for a nesting-place, tried to effect an entrance into the interior of a horizontal timber upon my porch, through a large crack. Not being able to do this, they brought straws and weed stalks and filled up the crack from one end of the porch to the other, working at it day after day notwithstanding their rubbish was repeatedly swept away. It was nesting-time, the opening in the timber stimulated them, and they kept going as did the birds I have mentioned above. I do not suppose they had any knowledge that their efforts were futile; they only had the impulse to build, and of that impulse they did not know the purpose.

I have not cited the foregoing incidents to show the stupidity of bird or beast or insect — that were as great an error as to seek to prove their reasoning powers — but simply to illustrate the automatic character of animal behavior; to show that, if the lower orders are not mere automata, as Des Cartes

187

long ago taught and as Huxley came to believe, adding only the qualifying adjective "conscious," making them "conscious automata," — then they come so near to it that it is difficult without exaggeration to credit them with any higher powers. At any rate, they reveal an order of mind that differs fundamentally from our own. Unless we are to abandon that comparison and classification which is the basis of all our knowledge, we must call it by another name — we must call it blind instinct. It does not see the why of anything which it does.

II

My dog and I are boon companions. I can live with him almost as with a brother, and yet I see him across a gulf. I catch a glimpse of that gulf, for example, when I see by his manner that he wants to lie down before the open fire, but, the poker or a stick of wood being in the way, instead of removing or pushing it to one side, as he could so easily do, he sits or half reclines there, and looks helplessly at the obstacle in his way. I get up and remove it and he lies down. The removal of that poker on his part would require a certain detachment and viewing of himself in relation to other things, of which he is not capable; and yet I know, had the obstacle barred the way to the retreat of a mouse or a chipmunk, he would have removed it in a hurry, because the scent of the game would have stimulated his instincts, or set up a reflex action, and put his paws in vigorous motion. He will, in an awkward kind of way, try to remove the burrs and bidens seeds from his coat, and bite at a sliver in his foot — these things irritate him and hence sustain a much closer relation to him than did the poker or the stick of wood; his instinct of self-defense is more or less aroused by them.

One's dog will come to cover when it rains, but can one think of him as putting on any cover to keep off the rain, or as bringing in his blanket out of the wet, unless especially trained? All such minor human acts are quite beyond the capacity of our wild or domestic animals, requiring as they do a certain self-detachment and viewing of things as they are in their relations.

Touch the spring of an animal's instinct or inherited habit, and it responds; but appeal to its power of independent thought, and it is, for the most part, as helpless as any other machine.

Birds will remove obstacles from their nests, and a setting hen will steal eggs from a nest within reach of her own. Such behavior shows only how acute and active their instincts are during the crisis of propagation.

The lower animals all seem to be upon the same plane; they are all yet at the breast of Nature, as it were, directly and unconsciously dependent upon her, while man has long since been weaned and separated from her. He has moved into another plane of being, still dependent, of course, upon the Nature of which he is, in a measure, the master. He still runs down into the region of reflex action, but he also runs up into the region of choice and reason and invention, where the animal does not follow him.

Man is emancipated, the animal is in bondage. And yet man surely came by the way of the lower animals. In these forms he tarried, these are his kith and kin; their marks are still upon him. But how he ever left them so far behind, who can tell? How did he cut loose from them? Why is my dog on one side of the gulf and I on the other? Why was he left behind by the impulse that brought me over? Why are we not either all dogs or all men? The wave has traveled, but the water has stayed behind. What started the wave? Where is the source of the force it represents? This man-impulse that has never been stayed, what or who started it? Through good and through evil report has it come, through slime and ooze, and reptile and fish, through monsters and dragons, and cat-aclysm, and cosmic winters and summers, and has arrived safely at last with man on its crest.

Of course the animals show many human traits; their whole emotional life — and it is doubtful if they have any other — seems to run parallel to our own. They live in feeling, not in thought. Huxley says that this is because they have no language.

190

REASONABLE BUT UNREASONING

They have no language because their brains are not developed to the language point. But to have emotions and feelings and associations and repulsions, the sense of direction, the sense of home, the love of offspring, the fear of enemies, we do not need a language, we need only the senses.

The animals show human traits every hour in the day, but my contention is that they do not show anything like human intelligence. The two pairs of orioles I saw one day come in collision as I was passing along the road behaved, I thought, in a very human way. Each couple had a nest in elm trees that stood near one another on the roadside, and were, of course, more or less jealous of each other's rights. As I was passing, the two females had come to blows in a clump of willows a few yards away and were having a lively scrap. Instantly the two males appeared, hurrying side by side to the scene of the squabble of their mates. Just what took place on their arrival I could not clearly make out, except that the females separated and the males came to blows. After sparring a moment or two, they alighted on the wire fence a few feet apart, where they eyed each other sharply and exchanged some very emphatic words, the purport of which I could only guess. How very human, I thought, that two husbands, in interfering in a quarrel between their wives, should get each other by the ears! My neighbor and I got into a "scrap" in trying to separate our dogs, exercising no more reason in the matter than did the orioles.

When Hobhouse, the English psychologist and philosopher, was trying to teach his elephant how to draw a bolt to open a box that contained a sweet morsel, the elephant used to lose its temper at times and bang the box around like a petulant child — a very human proceeding, I thought.

My son had a duck that one fall behaved, as it seemed to me, in quite a human way. He had a wild strain in him, and was brought up near the sea. He had lost his mate during the summer, and when fall came, I suppose the migrating instinct began to stir in him. He seemed uneasy and would leave the hens and wander off alone, softly calling as he walked. One night in early October he was missing, and we fancied a fox had snapped him up in the twilight. Days passed, till one evening one of the men saw a solitary duck flying past low over the buildings and fruit trees upon the lawn. He said it looked like our lost duck. A few days later the report came from our neighbor of a very tame wild duck upon the river. The duck had come ashore near his house, and he, not having a gun, had tried to capture it by a slip-noose at the end of a pole. But the duck took fright and flew away down the river. A day or two later it appeared again near our neighbor's house, and now, having learned that it was probably our lost duck, our neighbor set out to capture it by the use of corn, and finally succeeded. He then clipped one wing and turned it loose. The drake, failing in his efforts to fly, was a changed bird; disaster made him think of home, and the next day at twilight he turned his steps thitherward. He came slowly laboring up the hill, very silent and humble, and allowed himself to be picked up. It was hardly the return of a prodigal, but it was the coming back of a humbled and disappointed wanderer.

III

Animal conduct parallels human conduct in many particulars, but to say that it is the result of the same mental processes is, I believe, to make a capital mistake. Why, inorganic nature often seems to copy human methods, too, as, for instance, in a natural bridge. Behold on what sound mechanical principles the rude arch or span is built up! Shall we therefore ascribe the faculty of reason to the rocks? Or behold how the mountain-walls are buttressed, the overhanging cliff supported — it is all good engineering. In nature such things are the inevitable result of irrefragable mechanical laws; with the lower animals they are the result of instinct; with man they are the result of reason.

I notice that when the phœbe-bird builds her nest on the steep surface of a ledge, she begins like

193

a true mechanic and widens her foundation gradually as she comes upward, till she has a shelf of mud wide enough to stand it on. It is all fit and well considered. We may think that the bird reasoned, and fail to see how inevitable all such things are in organic as well as in inorganic nature. The trees buttress themselves at their base by a circle of high curving roots, and how their branches are braced and reinforced where they leave the trunk!

The beaver building its dam seems like a reasonable being, and L. H. Morgan, who studied this animal in its native haunts in Wisconsin, and wrote the best monograph upon the subject that has ever appeared, thinks that it does reason; but one incident alone which he mentions shows by what unreasoning instinct the animal is guided. He saw where the beavers had built a dam by the trunk of a tree that had fallen across a stream, but instead of placing their sticks and brush against the upper side of the tree, so as to avail themselves of it in resisting the force of the current, they had placed them below it, so that the tree helped them not at all. Poor things! they encountered a new problem. They could build a dam, but they could not take advantage of the aid which the wind had offered them. Probably, had they felled the tree themselves, their instinct would not have blundered so in dealing with it.

As animals get along very well without hands

and tools, so they get along very well without reason. Nature has given them tools in their organization in a sense that she has not given them to man — special appliances developed to meet special needs, such as hooks, spears, saws, files, chisels, barbs, drills, shears, probes, stings, drums, fiddles, cymbals, harps, glues, pastes, armors, stilts, pouches, all related to some need of the creature's life; and in the same way she has given them the quality of reason in their instincts. She has given the beaver knives and chisels in his teeth, she has given the woodpeckers drills in their beaks, she has given the leaf-cutters shears in their mandibles, she has given the bees baskets on their hips, she has given stilts to the waders and bills that are spears, to birds of prey claws that are hooks, and to various creatures weapons of offense and defense that man cannot boast of. Man has no tools or ornamental appendages in his organization, but he has that which can make and use these things — arms and hands, and reason to back them up. I can crack my nut with a stone or hammer, but the squirrel has teeth that help him to the kernel. Each of us is armed as best suits his needs. The mink and the otter can take their fish in the water, but I have to have a net, or a hook, or a weapon of some kind when I catch fish. The woodpecker can chisel out a hole in a tree for his nest or his house, with only the weapon nature gave him, but he cannot make a door to it, or patch it if it becomes leaky. The trap-door spider can build a door to her den, because this instinct is one of her special equipments, and is necessary to her well-being. To the woodpecker such a door is not a necessity.

There are but few things we could teach the animals in their own proper sphere. We could give them hints when they are confronted by new problems, as in the case of the beaver above referred to, but in the ordinary course of nature these new problems rarely turn up. We could teach the beaver a little more system in the use of his material, but this would be of slight value to him; his dam, made very much as a flood makes a dam of driftwood and mud, answers his purpose. Could we teach the birds where to find a milder clime, or the dog how to find his way home, or the horse how to find water in the desert, or the muskrat or the beaver how to plan and construct houses better suited to their purposes? Could we teach the birds how better to hide their nests? Do the conies amid the rocks, that cure their hay before storing it up for winter use, need to take counsel of us? or the timid hare that sleeps with its eyes open, or the sluggish turtle that covers her eggs in the warm sand? Can we instruct the honey-bee in her own arts, or the ant in hers? The spider does not need to learn of us how to weave a net, nor the leaf-rolling insect to be taught the use of stitches. I do not know that we first learned the art of paper-making from the hornets, but certain it is that they hold the original patent for making paper from wood-pulp; and the little spiders navigated the air before the first balloon was made, and the *Physalia* hoisted her sail long before the first seaman spread his, and the ant-lion dug his pit and the carpenter-bee bored his hole long before man had learned these arts. Indeed, many of the arts and crafts of man exist or are foreshadowed in the world of life below him. There is no tool-user among the lower animals that I know of, unless we regard one of the solitary wasps as such when she uses a pebble with which to pack down the earth over her den; but there are many curious devices and makeshifts of one kind and another among both plants and animals for defense, for hiding, for scattering of seeds, for cross-fertilization, etc. The wild creatures have all been to school to an old and wise teacher, Dame Nature, who has been keeping school now, as near as we can calculate, for several million years. And she is not an indulgent teacher, though a very patient one. Her rod is tooth and claw and hunger and cold and drought and flood, and her penalty is usually death. Her ways are not all ways of pleasantness, nor are all her paths paths of peace.

When the animals are confronted by conditions made by man, then man can give them valuable hints. We could teach the cliff swallows better than to stick their mud nests on boards that have been planed and painted, because sooner or later they are sure to fall. We could teach the cunning crow not to be afraid of a string stretched across the cornfield, and the wary fox not to be barred from a setting fowl by a hoop of iron, and we could teach him to elude the hounds by taking to the highway and jumping into the hind end of a passing farm wagon on the way to the mill and curling up among the meal-bags, as Mr. Roberts's fox did. We could instruct the bird with broken legs how to make clay casts for them, and to give the clay a chance to harden, as the woodcock of Dr. Long did. The wild animals do not need our medicine because they are probably never ill, and only upon very rare occasions could our surgery be of use to them. The domestic animals sometimes need a midwife, but probably the wild creatures never do. They all learn slowly the things that it is necessary for them to know. In time, I have no doubt, the migrating birds will learn to avoid the lighthouses along the coast, where so many of them now meet their death.

Animals know what they have to know in order that the species may continue, and they know little else. They do not have to reason because they do not progress as man does. They have only to live and multiply, and for this their instincts suffice them. Neither do they require any of our moral sentiments. These would be a hindrance rather than a help, and, so far as I can see, they do not have them.

X

THE GRIST OF THE GODS

ABOUT all we have in mind when we think of the earth is this thin pellicle of soil with which the granite framework of the globe is clothed — a red and brown film of pulverized and oxidized rock, scarcely thicker, relatively, than the paint or enamel which some women put on their cheeks, and which the rains often wash away as a tear washes off the paint and powder. But it is the main thing to us. Out of it we came and unto it we return. "Earth to earth, and dust to dust." The dust becomes warm and animated for a little while, takes on form and color, stalks about recuperating itself from its parent dust underfoot, and then fades and is resolved into the original earth elements. We are built up out of the ground quite as literally as the trees are, but not quite so immediately. The vegetable is between us and the soil, but our dependence is none the less real. "As common as dust" is one of our sayings, but the common, the universal, is always our mainstay in this world. When we see the dust turned into fruit and flowers and grain by that intangible thing called vegetable life, or into the bodies of men and women by the equally mysterious agency of animal life, we think better of it. The trembling gold of the pond-lily's heart, and its petals like carved snow, are no more a transformation of a little black muck and ooze by the chemistry of the sunbeam than our bodies and minds, too, are a transformation of the soil underfoot.

We are rooted to the air through our lungs and to the soil through our stomachs. We are walking trees and floating plants. The soil which in one form we spurn with our feet, and in another take into our mouths and into our blood — what a composite product it is! It is the grist out of which our bread of life is made, the grist which the mills of the gods, the slow patient gods of Erosion, have been so long grinding — grinding probably more millions of years than we have any idea of. The original stuff, the pulverized granite, was probably not very nourishing, but the fruitful hand of time has made it so. It is the kind of grist that improves with the keeping, and the more the meal-worms have worked in it, the better the bread. Indeed, until it has been eaten and digested by our faithful servitors the vegetables, it does not make the loaf that is our staff of life. The more death has gone into it, the more life comes out of it; the more it is a cemetery, the more it becomes a nursery; the more the rocks perish, the more the fields flourish.

This story of the soil appeals to the imagination.

THE GRIST OF THE GODS

To have a bit of earth to plant, to hoe, to delve in, is a rare privilege. If one stops to consider, one cannot turn it with his spade without emotion. We look back with the mind's eye through the vista of geologic time and we see islands and continents of barren, jagged rocks, not a grain of soil anywhere. We look again and behold a world of rounded hills and fertile valleys and plains, depth of soil where before were frowning rocks. The hand of time with its potent fingers of heat, frost, cloud, and air has passed slowly over the scene, and the miracle is done. The rocks turn to herbage, the fetid gases to the breath of flowers. The mountain melts down into a harvest field; volcanic scoria changes into garden mould; where towered a cliff now basks a green slope; where the strata yawned now bubbles a fountain; where the earth trembled, verdure now undulates. Your lawn and your meadow are built up of the ruins of the foreworld. The leanness of granite and gneiss has become the fat of the land. What transformation and promotion! — the decrepitude of the hills becoming the strength of the plains, the decay of the heights resulting in the renewal of the valleys!

Many of our hills are but the stumps of mountains which the hand of time has cut down. Hence we may say that if God made the mountains, time made the hills.

What adds to the wonder of the earth's grist is

that the millstones that did the work and are still doing it are the gentle forces that career above our heads — the sunbeam, the cloud, the air, the frost. The rain's gentle fall, the air's velvet touch, the sun's noiseless rays, the frost's exquisite crystals, these combined are the agents that crush the rocks and pulverize the mountains, and transform continents of sterile granite into a world of fertile soils. It is as if baby fingers did the work of giant powder and dynamite. Give the clouds and the sunbeams time enough, and the Alps and the Andes disappear before them, or are transformed into plains where corn may grow and cattle graze. The snow falls as softly as down and lies almost as lightly, yet the crags crumble beneath it; compacted by gravity, out of it grew the tremendous ice sheet that ground off the mountain summits, that scooped out lakes and valleys, and modeled our northern landscapes as the sculptor his clay image.

Not only are the mills of the gods grinding here, but the great cosmic mill in the sidereal heavens is grinding also, and some of its dust reaches our planet. Cosmic dust is apparently falling on the earth at all times. It is found in the heart of hailstones and in Alpine snows, and helps make up the mud of the ocean floors.

During the unthinkable time of the revolution of the earth around the sun, the amount of cosmic matter that has fallen upon its surface from out the depths of space must be enormous. It certainly must enter largely into the composition of the soil and of the sedimentary rocks. Celestial dirt we may truly call it, star dust, in which we plant our potatoes and grain and out of which Adam was made, and every son of man since Adam — the divine soil in very fact, the garden of the Eternal, contributed to by the heavens above and all the vital forces below, incorruptible, forever purifying itself, clothing the rocky framework of the globe as with flesh and blood, making the earth truly a mother with a teeming fruitful womb, and her hills veritable mammary glands. The iron in the fruit and vegetables we eat, which thence goes into our blood, may, not very long ago, have formed a part of the cosmic dust that drifted for untold ages along the highways of planets and suns.

The soil underfoot, or that we turn with our plow, how it thrills with life or the potencies of life! What a fresh, good odor it exhales when we turn it with our spade or plow in spring! It is good. No wonder children and horses like to eat it!

How inert and dead it looks, yet what silent, potent fermentations are going on there — millions and trillions of minute organisms ready to further your scheme of agriculture or horticulture. Plant your wheat or your corn in it, and behold the miracle of a birth of a plant or a tree. How it pushes up, fed and stimulated by the soil, through the agency of heat and moisture! It makes visible to the eye the life that is latent or held in suspense there in the cool, impassive ground. The acorn, the chestnut, the maple keys, have but to lie on the surface of the moist earth to feel its power and send down rootlets to meet it.

From one point of view, what a ruin the globe is! — worn and crumbled and effaced beyond recognition, had we known it in its youth. Where once towered mountains are now only their stumps — low, fertile hills or plains. Shake down your great city with its skyscrapers till most of its buildings are heaps of ruins with grass and herbage growing upon them, and you have a hint of what has happened to the earth.

Again, one cannot but reflect what a sucked orange the earth will be in the course of a few more centuries. Our civilization is terribly expensive to all its natural resources; one hundred years of modern life doubtless exhausts its stores more than a millennium of the life of antiquity. Its coal and oil will be about used up, all its mineral wealth greatly depleted, the fertility of its soil will have been washed into the sea through the drainage of its cities, its wild game will be nearly extinct, its primitive forests gone, and soon how nearly bankrupt the planet will be!

There is no better illustration of the way decay

and death play into the hands of life than the soil underfoot. The earth dies daily and has done so through countless ages. But life and youth spring forever from its decay; indeed, could not spring at all till the decay began. All the soil was once rock, perhaps many times rock, as the water that flows by may have been many times ice.

The soft, slow, aerial forces, how long and patiently they have worked! Oxygen has played its part in the way of oxidation and dioxidation of minerals. Carbon or carbonic acid has played its part, hydrogen has played its. Even granite yields slowly but surely to the action of rain-water. The sun is of course the great dynamo that runs the earth machinery and, through moisture and the air currents, reduces the rocks to soil. Without solar heat we should have no rain, and without rain we should have no soil. The decay of a mountain makes a hill of fertile fields. The soil, as we know it, is the product of three great processes — mechanical, chemical, and vital — which have been going on for untold ages. The mechanical we see in the friction of winds and waves and the grinding of glaciers, and in the destructive effects of heat and cold upon the rocks; the chemical in the solvent power of rain-water and of water charged with various acids and gases. The soil is rarely the color of the underlying rock from which it came, by reason of the action of the various gases of the atmosphere. Iron is black, but when turned into rust by the oxygen of the air, it is red.

The vital processes that have contributed to the soil we see going on about us in the decay of animal and vegetable matter. It is this process that gives the humus to the soil, in fact, almost humanizes it, making it tender and full of sentiment and memories, as it were, so that it responds more quickly to our needs and to our culture. The elements of the soil remember all those forms of animal and vegetable life of which they once made a part, and they take them on again the more readily. Hence the quick action of wood ashes upon vegetable life. Iron and lime and phosphorus that have once been taken up by growing plants and trees seem to have acquired new properties, and are the more readily taken up again.

The soil, like mankind, profits by experience, and grows deep and mellow with age. Turn up the cruder subsoil to the sun and air and to vegetable life, and after a time its character is changed; it becomes more gentle and kindly and more fertile.

All things are alike or under the same laws — the rocks, the soil, the soul of man, the trees in the forest, the stars in the sky. We have fertility, depth, geniality, in the ground underfoot, on the same terms upon which we have these things in human life and character.

We hardly realize how life itself has stored up

life in the soil, how the organic has wedded and blended with the inorganic in the ground we walk upon. Many if not all of the sedimentary rocks that were laid down in the abysms of the old ocean, out of which our soil has been produced, and that are being laid down now, out of which future soils will be produced, were and are largely of organic origin, the leavings of untold myriads of minute marine animals that lived millions of years ago. Our limestone rocks, thousands of feet thick in places, the decomposition of which furnishes some of our most fertile soils, are mainly of plant and animal origin. The chalk hills of England, so smooth and plump, so domestic and mutton-suggesting, as Huxley says, are the leavings of minute creatures called *Globigerinæ*, that lived and died in the ancient seas in the remote past. Other similar creatures, *Radiolaria* and diatoms, have played an equally important part in contributing the foundation of our soils. Diatom earth is found in places in Virginia forty feet thick. The coral insects have also contributed their share to the soil-making rocks. Our marl-beds, our phosphatic and carbonaceous rocks, are all largely of animal origin. So that much of our soil has lived and died many times, and has been charged more and more during the geologic ages or eternities with the potencies of life.

Indeed, Huxley, after examining the discoveries of the *Challenger* expedition, says there are good grounds for the belief " that all the chief known constituents of the crust of the earth may have formed part of living bodies; that they may be the ' ash' of protoplasm."

This implies that life first appeared in the sea, and gave rise to untold myriads of minute organisms, that built themselves shells out of the mineral matter held in solution by the water. As these organisms perished, their shells fell to the bottom and formed the sedimentary rocks. In the course of ages these rocks were lifted up above the sea, and their decay and disintegration under the action of the elements formed our soil — our clays, our marls, our green sand — and out of this soil man himself is built up.

I do not wonder that the Creator found the dust of the earth the right stuff to make Adam of. It was half man already. I can easily believe that his spirit was evoked from the same stuff, that it was latent there, and in due time, under the brooding warmth of the creative energy, awoke to life.

If matter is eternal, as science leads us to believe, and creation and recreation a never-ending process, then the present world, with all its myriad forms of the organic and the inorganic, is only one of the infinite number of forms that matter must have assumed in past æons. The whole substance of the globe must have gone to the making of other globes such a number of times as no array of figures could express. Every one of the sixty or more primary elements that make up our own bodies and the solid earth beneath us must have played the same part in the drama of life and death, growth and decay, organic and inorganic, that it is playing now, and will continue to play through an unending future.

This gross matter seems ever ready to vanish into the transcendental. When the new physics is done with it, what is there left but spirit, or something akin to it? When the physicist has followed matter through all its transformations, its final disguise seems to be electricity. The solid earth is resolvable into electricity, which comes as near to spirit as anything we can find in the universe.

Our senses are too dull and coarse to apprehend the subtle and incessant play of forces about us — the finer play and emanations of matter that go on all about us and through us. From a lighted candle, or gas-jet, or glowing metal shoot corpuscles or electrons, the basic constituents of matter, of inconceivable smallness — a thousand times smaller than an atom of hydrogen — and at the inconceivable speed of 10,000 to 90,000 miles a second. Think how we are bombarded by these bullets as we sit around the lamp or under the gas-jet at night, and are all unconscious of them! We are immersed in a sea of forces and potentialities of which we hardly dream. Of the scale of temperatures, from absolute zero to the heat of the sun, human life knows only a minute fraction. So of the elemental play of forces about us and over us, terrestrial and celestial —too fine for our apprehension on the one hand, and too large on the other — we know but a fraction.

The quivering and the throbbing of the earth under our feet in changes of temperature, the bendings and oscillations of the crust under the tread of the great atmospheric waves, the vital fermentations and oxidations in the soil — are all beyond the reach of our dull senses. We hear the wind in the treetops, but we do not hear the humming of the sap in the trees. We feel the pull of gravity, but we do not feel the medium through which it works. During the solar storms and disturbances all our magnetic and electrical instruments are agitated, but you and I are all unconscious of the agitation.

There are no doubt vibrations from out the depths of space that might reach our ears as sound were they attuned to the ether as the eye is when it receives a ray of light. We might hear the rush of the planets along their orbits, we might hear the explosions and uprushes in the sun; we might hear the wild whirl and dance of the nebulæ, where suns and systems are being formed; we might hear the "wreck of matter and the crush of worlds" that evidently takes place now and then in the abysms of space, because all these things must send through the ether impulses and tremblings that reach our planet. But if we felt or heard or saw or were conscious of all that was going on in the universe, what a state of agitation we should be in! Our scale of apprehension is wisely limited, mainly to things that concern our well-being.

But let not care and humdrum deaden us to the wonders and the mysteries amid which we live, nor to the splendors and the glories. We need not translate ourselves in imagination to some other sphere or state of being to find the marvelous, the divine, the transcendent; we need not postpone our day of wonder and appreciation to some future time and condition. The true inwardness of this gross visible world, hanging like an apple on the bough of the great cosmic tree, and swelling with all the juices and potencies of life, transcends anything we have dreamed of super-terrestrial abodes. It is because of these things, because of the vitality, spirituality, oneness, and immanence of the universe as revealed by science, its condition of transcending time and space, without youth and without age, neither beginning nor ending, neither material nor spiritual, but forever passing from one into the other, that I was early and deeply impressed by Walt Whitman's lines: —

"There was never any more inception than there is now,
    Nor any more youth or age than there is now;
    And will never be any more perfection than there is now,
    Nor any more heaven or hell than there is now."

And I may add, nor any more creation than there is now, nor any more miracles, or glories, or wonders, or immortality, or judgment days, than there are now. And we shall never be nearer God and spiritual and transcendent things than we are now. The babe in its mother's womb is not nearer its mother than we are to the invisible sustaining and mothering powers of the universe, and to its spiritual entities, every moment of our lives.

The doors and windows of the universe are all open; the screens are all transparent. We are not barred or shut off; there is nothing foreign or unlike; we find our own in the stars as in the ground underfoot; this clod may become a man; yon shooting star may help redden his blood.

Whatever is upon the earth is of the earth; it came out of the divine soil, beamed upon by the fructifying heavens, the soul of man not less than his body.

I never see the spring flowers rising from the mould, or the pond-lilies born of the black ooze, that matter does not become transparent and reveal to me the working of the same celestial powers that fashioned the first man from the common dust.

Man's mind is no more a stranger to the earth than is his body. Is not the clod wise? Is not the chemistry underfoot intelligent? Do not the roots of the trees find their way? Do not the birds know their times and seasons? Are not all things about us filled to overflowing with mind-stuff? The cosmic mind is the earth mind, and the earth mind is man's mind, freed but narrowed, with vision but with erring reason, conscious but troubled, and — shall we say? — human but immortal.

XI

THE DIVINE SOIL

I

HOW few persons can be convinced of the truth of that which is repugnant to their feelings! When Darwin published his conclusion that man was descended from an apelike ancestor who was again descended from a still lower type, most people were shocked by the thought; it was intensely repugnant to their feelings. Carlyle, for instance, treated the proposition with contempt. He called it the "gospel of dirt." "A good sort of man," he said, "is this Darwin, and well meaning, but with very little intellect." Huxley tells of seeing the old man one day upon the street, and of crossing over to greet him. Carlyle looked up and said, "You're Huxley, are n't you? the man who says we are all descended from monkeys," and went on his way. It would be interesting to know just what Carlyle thought we were descended from. Could he, or did he, doubt at all that if he were to go back a few thousand years over his own line of descent, he would come upon rude savage men, who used stone implements, and lived in caves or rude huts, who had neither letters nor arts, and with whom might did indeed make right, and that back of these he would find

215

still more primitive races, and that these too had their still more savage and bestial forbears? When started on the back track of his own race, where could he stop? Could he stop anywhere? The neolithic man stands on the shoulders of the paleolithic, and he on a still lower human or semi-human form, till we come to a manlike ape or an apelike man, living in trees and subsisting on roots and nuts and wild fruits. Every child born to-day, by the grip of its hands, the strength of its arms, and the weakness of its legs, hints of those far-off arboreal ancestors. Carlyle must also have known that in his fetal or prenatal life there was a time when his embryo could not have been distinguished from that of a dog, to say nothing of a monkey. Was this fact also intolerable to him?

It must be a bitter pill to persons of Carlyle's temperament to have to accept the account of their own human origin; that the stork legend of the baby is, after all, not good natural history. The humble beginning of each of us is not one that appeals to the imagination, nor to the religious sentiment, nor to our love of the mysterious and the remote, yet the evidence in favor of its truth is pretty strong.

In fact, the Darwinian theory of the origin of man differs from the popular one just as the natural history of babies as we all know it differs from the account in the nursery legends, and gives about

the same shock to our sensibilities and our pride
of origin.

One of the hardest lessons we have to learn in
this life, and one that many persons never learn,
is to see the divine, the celestial, the pure, in the
common, the near at hand — to see that heaven
lies about us here in this world. Carlyle's gospel
of dirt, when examined closely, differs in no respect
from a gospel of star dust. Why, we have invented
the whole machinery of the supernatural, with its
unseen spirits and powers good and bad, to account
for things, because we found the universal every-
day nature too cheap, too common, too vulgar. We
have had to cap the natural with the supernatural
to satisfy our love for the marvelous and the inexplicable. As soon as a thing is brought within our
ken and the region of our experience, it seems to
lose caste and be cheapened. I am at a loss how to
account for this mythopoetic tendency of ours, but
what a part it has played in the history of mankind,
and what a part it still plays — turning the light
of day into a mysterious illusive and haunted twilight on every hand! It would seem as if it must
have served some good purpose in the development
of the race, but just what is not so easy to point out
as the evil it has wrought, the mistakes and self-
delusions it has given rise to. One may probably
say that in its healthy and legitimate action it has
given rise to poetry and to art and to the many

escapes which the imagination provides us from the hard and wearing realities of life. Its implacable foe is undoubtedly the scientific spirit — the spirit of the now and the here, that seeks proof and finds the marvelous and the divine in the ground underfoot; the spirit that animated Lyell and opened his eyes to the fact that the forces and agencies at work every day around us were adequate to account for the tremendous changes in the earth's surface in the past; that animated Darwin and led him to trace the footsteps of the creative energy in the natural life of plants and animals to-day; that animated Huxley and filled him with such righteous wrath at the credulity of his theological brethren; and that animates every one of us when we clinch a nail, or stop a leak, or turn a thing over and look on the other side, and apply to practical affairs the touchstone of common sense.

That man is of divine origin in a sense that no other animal is, is a conviction dear to the common mind. It was dear to the mind of Carlyle, it chimed in well with his distrust of the present, his veneration of the past, and his Hebraic awe and reverential fear before the mysteries of the universe. While Darwin's attitude of mind toward outward things was one of inquiry and thirst for exact knowledge, Carlyle's was one of reverence and wonder. He was more inclined to worship where Darwin was moved to investigate. Darwin, too, felt the presence of the great unknown, but he sought solace in the knowable of the physical world about him, while Carlyle sought solace in the moral and intellectual world, where his great mythopoetic faculty could have free swing.

We teach and we preach that God is in everything from the lowest to the highest, and that all things are possible with him, and yet practically we deny that he is in the brute, and that it is possible man should have had his origin there.

I long ago convinced myself that whatever is on the earth and shares its life is of the earth, and, in some way not open to me, came out of the earth, the highest not less than the humblest creature at our feet. I like to think of the old weather-worn globe as the mother of us all. I like to think of the ground underfoot as plastic and responsive to the creative energy, vitally related to the great cosmic forces, a red corpuscle in the life current of the Eternal, and that man, with all his high-flying dreams and aspirations, his arts, his bibles, his religions, his literatures, his philosophies — heroes, saints, martyrs, sages, poets, prophets — all lay folded there in the fiery mist out of which the planet came. I love to make Whitman's great lines my own: —

"I am an acme of things accomplished, and I an endorser of
      things to be.
My feet strike an apex of the apices of the stairs,

On every step bunches of ages, and larger bunches between
    the steps,
All below duly traveled, and still I mount and mount.

" Rise after rise bow the phantoms behind me,
Afar down I see the huge first Nothing — I know I was even
    there,
I waited unseen and always, and slept through the lethargic
    mist,
And took my time, and took no hurt from the fetid carbon.

" Long I was hugged close — long and long.
Immense have been the preparations for me,
Faithful and friendly the arms that have helped me.
Cycles ferried my cradle, rowing and rowing like cheerful boat-
    men,
For room to me stars kept aside in their own rings,
They sent influences to look after what was to hold me.

" Before I was born out of my mother generations guided me,
My embryo has never been torpid — nothing could overlay it.
For it the nebula cohered to an orb,
The long, slow strata piled to rest it in,
Vast vegetables gave it sustenance,
Monstrous sauroids transported it in their mouths and depos-
    ited it with care.
All forces have been steadily employed to complete and delight
    me,
Now I stand on this spot with my Soul."

II

The material, the carnal, the earthy, has been so
long under the ban, so long associated in our minds
with that which hinders and degrades, and as the
source and province of evil, that it will take sci-

ence a long time to redeem it and lift it again to its proper place.

It jars upon our sensibilities and disturbs our preconceived notions to be told that the spiritual has its root in the carnal, and is as truly its product as the flower is the product of the roots and the stalk of the plant. The conception does not cheapen or degrade the spiritual, it elevates the carnal, the material. To regard the soul and body as one, or to ascribe to consciousness a physiological origin, is not detracting from its divinity, it is rather conferring divinity upon the body. One thing is inevitably linked with another — the higher forms with the lower forms, the butterfly with the grub, the flower with the root, the food we eat with the thought we think, the poem we write, or the picture we paint, with the processes of digestion and nutrition. How science has enlarged and ennobled and purified our conception of the universe; how it has cleaned out the evil spirits that have so long terrified mankind, and justified the verdict of the Creator: "and behold it was good"! With its indestructibility of matter, its conservation of energy, its inviolability of cause and effect, its unity of force and elements throughout sidereal space, it has prepared the way for a conception of man, his origin, his development, and in a measure his destiny, that at last makes him at home in the universe.

How much more consistent it is with what we

know of the unity of nature to believe that one species should have come through another, that man should have come through the brute rather than have been grafted upon him from without. Unfolding and ever unfolding, upward and onward, from the lower to the higher, from the simple to the complex — that has been the course of organic evolution from the first.

One thinks of the creative energy as working along many lines, only one of which eventuated in man; all the others fell short, or terminated in lower forms. Hence while we think of man as capable of, and destined to, still higher development, we look upon the lower orders as having reached the end of their course, and conclude there is no to-morrow for them.

The anthropoid apes seem indeed like preliminary studies of man, or rejected models of the great inventor who was blindly groping his way to the higher form. The ape is probably our ancestor in no other sense than this. Nature seems to have had man in mind when she made him, but evidently she lost interest in him, humanly speaking, and tried some other combination. The ape must always remain an ape. Some collateral branch doubtless gave birth to a higher form, and this to a still higher, till we reach our preglacial forbears. Then some one branch or branches distanced all others, leaving rude tribes by the way in whom development seemed arrested, till we reach the dawn of history.

The creative energy seems ever to have been pushing out and on, and yet ever leaving a residue of forms behind. The reptiles did not all become birds, nor the invertebrates all become vertebrates, nor the apes all become men, nor the men all become Europeans. Every higher form has a base or background of kindred lower forms out of which it seems to have emerged, and to which it now and then shows a tendency to revert. And this is the order of nature everywhere, in our own physiology and psychology not less than in the evolution of the forms of life. Do not our highest ideals have their rise and foundation in sensation and experience ? There is no higher without first the lower, and the lower does not all become the higher.

The blood relationship between man and the anthropoid apes, as shown in the fact that human blood acts poisonously upon and decomposes the blood of the lower apes and other mammals, but is harmless to the blood of the anthropoid apes and affiliates with it, is very significant. It convinces like a demonstration. Transfer the blood of the dog to the fox or the wolf, or *vice versa*, and all goes well; they are brothers. Transfer the blood of the dog to the rabbit, or *vice versa*, and a struggle for life immediately takes place. The serum of one blood destroys the cells of the other. This fact confirms Huxley's statement that the anatomical difference between man and the anthropoid apes is less than the corresponding difference between the latter and the lower apes.

III

One thing we may affirm about the universe — it is logical; the conclusion always follows from the premises.

The lesson which life repeats and constantly enforces is "look under foot." You are always nearer the divine and the true sources of your power than you think. The lure of the distant and the difficult is deceptive. The great opportunity is where you are. Do not despise your own place and hour. Every place is under the stars, every place is the centre of the world. Stand in your own dooryard and you have eight thousand miles of solid ground beneath you, and all the sidereal splendors overhead. The morning and the evening stars are no more in the heavens and no more obedient to the celestial impulses than the lonely and time-scarred world we inhabit. How the planet thrills and responds to the heavenly forces and occurrences we little know, but we get an inkling of it when we see the magnetic needle instantly affected by solar disturbances.

Look under foot. Gold and diamonds and all

precious stones come out of the ground; they do not drop upon us from the stars, and our highest thoughts are in some way a transformation or a transmutation of the food we eat. The mean is the divine if we make it so. The child surely learns that its father and mother are the Santa Claus that brought the gifts, though the discovery may bring pain; and the man learns to see providence in the great universal forces of nature, in the winds and the rain, in the soil underfoot and in the cloud over-head. What these forces in their orderly rounds do not bring him, he does not expect. The farmer hangs up his stocking in the way of empty bins and barns, and he knows well who or what must fill them. The Santa Claus of the merchant, the manu-facturer, the inventor, is the forces and conditions all about us in every-day operation. When the light-ning strikes your building or the trees on your lawn, you are at least reminded that you do not live in a corner outside of Jove's dominions, you are in the circuit of the great forces. If you are eligible to bad fortune where you stand, you are equally eligible to good fortune there. The young man who went West did well, but the young man who had the Western spirit and stayed at home did equally well. To evoke a spark of fire out of a flint with a bit of steel is the same thing as evoking beautiful thoughts from homely facts. How hard it is for us to see the heroic in an act of our neighbor!

IV

What a burden science took upon itself when it sought to explain the origin of man! Religion or theology takes a short cut and makes quick work of it by regarding man as the result of the special creative act of a supernatural Being. But science takes a long and tedious and hazardous way around through the lowest primordial forms of life. It seeks to trace his germ through the abyss of geologic time, where all is dim and mysterious, through countless cycles of waiting and preparation, where the slow, patient gods of evolution cherished it and passed it on, through the fetid carbon, through the birth and decay of continents, through countless interchanges and readjustments of sea and land, through the clash and warring of the cosmic forces, through good and evil report, through the fish and the reptile, through the ape and the orang, up to man — from the slime at the bottom of the primordial ocean up to Jesus of Nazareth. Surely one may say with Whitman, —

> "Immense have been the preparations for me,
> Faithful and friendly the arms that have helped me."

It took about one hundred thousand feet of sedimentary rock, laid down through hundreds of millions of years in the bottom of the old seas, all probably the leavings of minute forms of life, to make a foundation upon which man could appear.

THE DIVINE SOIL

His origin as revealed by science fills and appalls the imagination: as revealed by theology it simply baffles and dumfounds one. Science deepens the mystery while yet it gives the reason and the imagination something to go upon; it takes us beyond soundings, but not beyond the assurance that cause and effect are still continuous there beneath us. I like to think that man has traveled that long, adventurous road, that the whole creation has pulled together to produce him. It is a road, of course, beset with pain and anguish, beset with ugly and repellent forms, beset with riot and slaughter; it leads through jungle and morass, through floods and cataclysms, through the hells of the Mesozoic and the Cenozoic periods, but it leads ever upward and onward.

The manward impulse in creation has doubtless been checked many times, but never lost; all forms conspired to further it, and it seemed to have taken the push and the aspiration out of each order as it passed on, dooming it henceforth to a round of life without change or hope of progress, leaving the fish to continue fish, the reptiles to continue reptiles, the apes to continue apes; it took all the heart and soul of each to feed and continue the central impulse that was to eventuate in man.

I fail to see why our religious brethren cannot find in this history or revelation as much room for creative energy, as large a factor of the mysterious and

superhuman, as in the myth of Genesis. True it is
that it fixes our attention upon this world and upon
forces with which we are more or less familiar, but
it implies an element or a power before which we
stand helpless and dumb. What fathered this man-
impulse, what launched this evolutionary process,
what or who stamped upon the first protoplasm
the aspiration to be man, and never let that aspiration sleep through all the tremendous changes of
those incalculable geologic ages? What or who first
planted the seed of the great biological tree, and
determined all its branchings and the fruit it should
bear? If you must have a God, either apart from
or imminent in creation, it seems to me that there
is as much need of one here as in the Mosaic cos-
mology. The final mystery cannot be cleared up.
We can only drive it to cover. How the universe
came to be what it is, and how man came to be
man, who can tell us?

That somewhere in my line of descent was an
ancestor that lived in trees and had powerful arms
and weaker legs, that his line began in a creature
that lived on the ground, and his in one that lived
in the mud, or in the sea, and his, or its, sprang
from a germ at the bottom of the sea, but deepens
the mystery of the being that is now here and can
look back and speculate over the course he has
probably come; it only directs attention to ugly
facts, to material things, to the every-day process

of evolution, instead of to the far away, the unknown, or the supernatural.

How the organic came to bud and grow from the
inorganic, who knows? Yet it must have done so.
We seem compelled to think of an ascending series
from nebular matter up to the spirituality of man,
each stage in the series resting upon or growing
out of the one beneath it. Creation or development must be continuous. There are and can be
no breaks. The inorganic is already endowed with
chemical and molecular life. The whole universe
is alive, and vibrates with impulses too fine for
our dull senses; but in chemical affinity, in crystallization, in the persistence of force, in electricity, we catch glimpses of a kind of vitality that
is preliminary to all other. I never see fire burn,
or water flow, or the frost-mark on the pane,
that I am not reminded of something as mysterious as life. How alive the flame seems, how
alive the water, how marvelous the arborescent etch-
ings of the frost! Is there a principle of fire?
Is there a principle of crystallization? Just as
much as there is a principle of life. The mind,
in each case, seems to require something to lay
hold of as a cause. Why these wonderful star
forms of the snowflake? Why these exact geo-
metric forms of quartz crystals? The gulf between
disorganized matter and the crystal seems to me
as great as that between the organic and the inor-

ganic. If we did not every day witness the passage, we could not believe it. The gulf between the crystal and the cell we have not seen cleared, and man has not yet been able to bridge it, and may never be, but it has been bridged, and I dare say without any more miracle than hourly goes on around us. The production of water from two invisible gases is a miracle to me. When water appeared (what made it appear?) and the first cloud floated across the blue sky, life was not far off, if it was not already there. Some morning in spring when the sun shone across the old Azoic hills, at some point where the land and sea met, life began — the first speck of protoplasm appeared. Call it the result of the throb or push of the creative energy that pervades all things, and whose action is continuous and not intermittent, since we are compelled to presuppose such energy to account for anything, even our own efforts to account for things. An ever active vital force pervades the universe, and is felt and seen in all things, from atomic attraction and repulsion up to wheeling suns and systems. The very processes of thought seem to require such premises to go upon. There is a reason for the universe as we find it, else man's reason is a delusion, and delusion itself is a meaningless term. The uncaused is unthinkable; thought can find neither beginning nor ending to the universe because it cannot find the primal cause. Can

we think of a stick with only one end? We have
to if we compass time in thought, or space, either.

v

Given atomic motion, chemical affinity — this
hunger or love of the elements for one another —
crystallization, electricity, radium, the raining upon
us of solar and sidereal influences, the youth of the
earth, and the whole universe vibrating with the cosmic creative energy, the beginning of life, the step
from the inorganic to the organic, is not so hard to
conceive. In a dead universe this would be hard,
but we have a universe throbbing with cosmic life
and passion to begin with. It is impossible for me
to think of anything as uncaused, and in trying to
figure to myself this beginning of life I have to
postulate this universal creative energy that pervades
the worlds as animating the atoms and causing
them to combine so as to produce the primordial
protoplasm. Then when the first cell divides and
becomes two, I have to think of an inherent something that prompts the act, and so on all the way up.

I cannot conceive of crystallization, this precise
and invariable arrangement of certain elements,
nor of the invariable chemical compounds, without
postulating some inner force, or will, or tendency
that determines them. I cannot conceive of an
atom of carbon, or oxygen, or hydrogen as doing
anything of itself. It must be alive, and this life

231

and purpose pervades the universe. This inability on my part may be only the limitation of thought. I know there are things I cannot conceive of that are yet true. I cannot conceive how the sky is still overhead at the South Pole as at the North, because one position to my senses is the reverse of the other, and I am compelled to think of up and down as the same. I cannot think how anything can begin, because time, like matter, is infinitely divisible, and there always remains a mathematical fragment of time between the not beginning and the beginning. The conditions of thought are such that I do not see how one can think of one's self, that is, be object and subject at the same instant of time — jump down one's own throat, so to speak — and yet we seem to manage to do it.

VI

If life can finally be explained in terms of physics and chemistry, that is, if the beginning of life upon the globe was no new thing, the introduction of no new principle, but only the result of a vastly more complex and intimate play and interaction of the old physico-chemical forces of the inorganic world, then the gulf that is supposed to separate the two worlds of living and non-living matter virtually disappears: the two worlds meet and fuse. We shall probably in time have to come to accept this view — the view of the mechanico-chemical theory of life.

THE DIVINE SOIL

It is in a line with the whole revelation of science, so far — the getting rid of the miraculous, the unknowable, the transcendental, and the enhancing of the potency and the mystery of things near at hand that we have always known in other forms. It is at first an unpalatable truth, like the discovery of the animal origin of man, or that consciousness and all our fine thoughts and aspirations are the result of molecular action in the brain; or like the experience of the child when it discovers that its father or mother is the Santa Claus that filled its stockings. Science is constantly bringing us back to earth and to the ground underfoot. Our dream of something far off, supernatural, vanishes. We lose the God of a far-off heaven, and find a God in the common, the near, always present, always active, always creating the world anew. Science thus corrects our delusions and vague superstitions, and brings us back near home for the key we had sought afar. We shall probably be brought, sooner or later, to accept another unpalatable theory, that of the physical origin of the soul, that it is not of celestial birth except as the celestial and terrestrial are one. This is really only taking our religious teachers at their word, that God is here, as constant and as active in the commonest substance we know as in the highest heaven. Science finds the beginning of something like conscious intelligence in the first unicellular life, the first pro-

tozoön. When two or more cells unite to form a
metazoön, it finds a higher and more complex form
of intelligence. In the brain of man it finds a confra-
ternity of millions of simple cells, each with a life and
intelligence of its own, but when united and coöp-
erating, the intelligence of all *pooled*, as it were, we
have the mind and personality of man as the result.
This fact leaves no room for the notion that the
mind or soul is an entity apart from the organ which
it uses. It seems, on the contrary, in some mysterious way to be the result of the multicellular life
of the nervous system. Thus we do not banish the
mystery of the soul, we only bring it nearer home.
We disprove a fable, and are then confounded by
the fact that lurks under it. And this proves true in
all attempts at ultimate explanations of the phenomena of this world.

It seems as if we saw the hint of prophecy of the
vegetable in the mineral — in this growth of crystals, in these arborescent forms of the frost on the
pane or on the flagging-stones. One may see most
wonderful tree and fern forms upon the pavement,
with clean open spaces between them, as much so
as in a wood, an endless variety of them. A French
chemist has lately produced by inorganic compounds the growth of something like a plant with
roots, stem, branches, leaves, buds — a mineral
plant, as if the type of the plant already existed
in the soil. Yes, the inorganic is dreaming of the

organic. And the plant in its cell structure, in its circulation, in its intelligence, or in its ingenious devices to get on in the world is dreaming of the animal, and the animal is dreaming of the spiritual, and the spirituality of man touches the spirituality of the cosmos, and thus the circle is complete.

VII

So far as science can find out, *sentience* is a property of matter which is evolved under certain conditions, and though science itself has not yet been able to reproduce these conditions, it still believes in the possibility. If life was not potential in the inorganic world, how is it possible to account for it? It is not a graft, it is more like a begetting. Nature does not work by prefixes and suffixes, but by unfolding and ever unfolding, or developing out of latent innate powers and possibilities; — an inward necessity always working, but never an external maker. It is no help to fancy that life may have been brought to the earth by a falling meteorite from some other sphere. How did life originate upon that other sphere? It must have started here as surely as fire started here. We feign that Prometheus stole the first fire from heaven, but it sleeps here all about us, and can be evoked any time and anywhere. It sleeps in all forms of force. A falling avalanche of rocks turns to flame; the meteor in the air becomes a torch;

the thunderbolt is a huge spark. So life, no doubt, slept in the inorganic, and was started by the reverse of friction, namely, by brooding.

When the earth becomes lifeless again, as it surely must in time, then the cycle will be repeated, a collision will develop new energy and new worlds, and out of this newness will again come life.

It is highly probable that a million years elapsed between the time when the ancestor of man began to assume the human form and the dawn of history. Try to think of that time and of the struggle of this creature upward; of the pain, the suffering, the low bestial life, the warrings, the defeats, the slow, infinitely slow gains, of his deadly enemies in other animals, of the repeated changes of climate of the northern hemisphere from subtropical to subarctic — the land at one time for thousands of years buried beneath an ice sheet a mile or more thick, followed by a cycle of years of almost tropical warmth even in Greenland — and all of this before man had yet got off of " all fours," and stood upright and began to make rude tools and rude shelters from the storms. The Tertiary period, early in which the first rude ancestor of man seems to have appeared, is less than one week of the great geologic year of the earth's history — a week of about five days. These days the geologists have named Eocene, Oligocene, Miocene, Pliocene, and Pleistocene, each one of these days covering, no doubt, a million years or more. The ancestor of man probably took on something like the human form on the third, or Miocene, day. The other and earlier fifty or more weeks of the great geologic year gradually saw the development of the simpler forms of life, till we reach the earliest mammals and reptiles in the Permian, about the forty-eighth or forty-ninth week of the great year. The laying down of the coal measures, Huxley thinks, must have taken six millions of years. Well, the Lord allowed himself enough time. Evidently he was in no hurry to see man cutting his fantastic tricks here upon the surface of the planet. A hundred million years, more or less, what of it? Did the globe have to ripen all those cycles upon cycles, like the apple upon the tree? bask in the sidereal currents, work and ferment in the sea of the hypothetical ether before the gross matter could evolve the higher forms of life? Probably every unicellular organism that lived and died in the old seas helped prepare the way for man, contributed something to the fund of vital energy of the globe upon which man was finally to draw.

How life has had to adjust itself to the great cosmic changes! The delays must have been incalculable. The periodic refrigeration of the northern hemisphere, which brought on the ice age several times during each one of the Eocene and Miocene days, must have delayed the development of life as we know it, enormously.

237

LEAF AND TENDRIL

VIII

From nebula to nebula — these are the hours struck by the clock of eternity : from the dissipation of the solar systems into nebular gas by their falling together to their condensation again into suns and worlds by the action of physical laws — thousands of millions of years in each hour, and the hours infinite in number. This is a hint of eternity. How many times, then, there must have been a world like this evolved in the course of this running down and winding up of the great clock, with beings like these we now behold! how many such worlds and such beings there must now be in the universe, and have always been! Can you think of the number? Not till you can think of infinity. The duration of life upon the globe, to say nothing of man's little span, is hardly a tick of this clock of eternity, and the repetition of the birth and dissipations of systems is well symbolized by the endless striking or ticking of a clock.

Then sooner or later comes the thought, What is it all for? and from the great abysm comes back the echo, "What for?" Is it our human limitations, the discipline of this earthly life, when we have to count the cost and ask what it is for, that makes us put the question to the Infinite? When the cosmic show is over, what is the gain? When our universe is again a blank, who or what will have reaped the benefit? Will the moral order which has been so slowly and painfully evolved, and which so · many souls have struggled to live up to, still go on? Where? with whom? I seem to see dimly that you cannot bring the Infinite to book, that you cannot ask, "What for?" of the All, — of that which has neither beginning nor end, neither centre nor circumference, neither fulfillment nor design, which knows neither failure nor success, neither loss nor gain, and which is complete in and of itself.

We are tied to the sphere, its laws shape our minds, we cannot get away from it and see it in perspective; away from it there is no direction; at either pole on its surface there is the contradiction of the sky being always overhead. We are tied to the Infinite in the same way. We are part of it, but may not measure it. Our boldest thought comes back like a projectile fired into the heavens — the curve of the infinite sphere holds us. I know I am trying to say the unsayable. I would fain indicate how human and hopeless is our question, "What for?" when asked of the totality of things. There is no totality of things. To say that there is, does not express it. To say there is not, does not express it. To say that the universe was created, does not express the mystery; to say that it was not created, but always existed, does not express it any nearer. To say that the heavens are overhead is only half the truth; they are underfoot also.

Down is toward the centre of the earth, but go on through and come out at the surface on the other side, and which way is down then?

The Unspeakable will not be spoken.

In the light of science we must see that life and progress and evolution and the moral order must go on and on somewhere, that the birth of systems and the evolution of planets must and does continue, and always has continued; that if one sun fades, another blazes out; that as there must have been an infinite number (how can there be an infinite number? where is the end of the endless?) of worlds in the past, so there will be an infinite number in the future; that if the moral order and the mathematical order and the intellectual order disappear from one planet, they will appear in due time on another.

All that which in our limited view of nature we call waste and delay — how can such terms apply to the Infinite? Can we ever speak truly of the Infinite in terms of the finite? To be sure, we have no other terms, and can never have. Then let us be silent and — reverent.

XII

AN OUTLOOK UPON LIFE

I

THIS chapter, with its personal and autobio-
graphical note, seems to call for some word
of explanation. A few years since, a magazine
editor asked me, as he asked others, to tell his
readers something of what life meant to me, basing
the paper largely upon my own personal experiences. The main part of the following essay was
the result. The paper was so well received by a
good many readers that, with some additions, I
have decided to include it in this collection.

I have had a happy life, and there is not much
of it I would change if I could live it over again.
I think I was born under happy stars, with a keen
sense of wonder, which has never left me, and which
only becomes jaded a little now and then, and with
no exaggerated notion of my own deserts. I have
shared the common lot, and have found it good
enough for me. Unlucky is the man who is born
with great expectations, and who finds nothing in
life quite up to the mark.

One of the best things a man can bring into the
world with him is natural humility of spirit. About

the next best thing he can bring, and they usually go together, is an appreciative spirit — a loving and susceptible heart. If he is going to be a reformer and stir up things, and slay the dragons, he needs other qualities more. But if he is going to get the most out of life in a worthy way, if he is going to enjoy the grand spectacle of the world from first to last, then he needs his life pitched in a low key and well attuned to common universal things. The strained, the loud, the far-fetched, the extravagant, the frenzied — how lucky we are to escape them, and to be born with dispositions that cause us to flee from them!

I would gladly chant a pæan for the world as I find it. What a mighty interesting place to live in! If I had my life to live over again, and had my choice of celestial abodes, I am sure I should take this planet, and I should choose these men and women for my friends and companions. This great rolling sphere with its sky, its stars, its sunrises and sunsets, and with its outlook into infinity — what could be more desirable? What more satisfying? Garlanded by the seasons, embosomed in sidereal influences, thrilling with life, with a heart of fire and a garment of azure seas, and fruitful continents — one might ransack the heavens in vain for a better or a more picturesque abode. As Emerson says, it is "well worth the heart and pith of great men to subdue and enjoy it."

AN OUTLOOK UPON LIFE

O to share the great, sunny, joyous life of the earth! to be as happy as the birds are! as contented as the cattle on the hills! as the leaves of the trees that dance and rustle in the wind! as the waters that murmur and sparkle to the sea! To be able to see that the sin and sorrow and suffering of the world are a necessary part of the natural course of things, a phase of the law of growth and development that runs through the universe, bitter in its personal application, but illuminating when we look upon life as a whole! Without death and decay, how could life go on? Without what we call sin (which is another name for imperfection) and the struggle consequent upon it, how could our development proceed? I know the waste, the delay, the suffering in the history of the race are appalling, but they only repeat the waste, the delay, the conflict through which the earth itself has gone and is still going, and which finally issues in peace and tranquillity. Look at the grass, the flowers, the sweet serenity and re-pose of the fields — at what a price it has all been bought, of what a warring of the elements, of what overturnings, and pulverizings and shiftings of land and sea, and slow grindings of the mills of the gods of the fore-world it is all the outcome!

The agony of Russia at the present time (1904), the fire and sword, the snapping of social and political ties, the chaos and destruction that seem imminent —what is it but a geologic upheaval, the price that must be paid for law and order on a permanent basis? We deplore the waste and the suffering, but these things never can be eliminated from the processes of evolution. As individuals we can mitigate them; as races and nations we have to endure them. Waste, pain, delay — the gods smile at these things; so that the game goes on, that is enough. How many thousand centuries of darkness and horror lie between the man of to-day and the low animal ancestor from which he sprang! Who can picture the sufferings and the defeats! But here we are, and all that terrible past is forgotten, is, as it were, the soil under our feet.

Our fathers were cheered and sustained by a faith in special providences — that there was a Supreme Power that specially interested itself in man and his doings, and that had throughout the course of history turned the adverse currents in his favor. It is certain that all things have worked together for the final good of the race as a whole, otherwise it would have disappeared from the face of the earth. But Providence does things by wholesale. It is like the rain that falls upon the sea and the land equally, upon the just and the unjust, where it is needed and where it is not needed; and the evolution of the life of the globe, including the life of man, has gone on and still goes on, because, in the conflict of forces, the influences that favored life and forwarded it have in the end triumphed.

AN OUTLOOK UPON LIFE

Our good fortune is not that there are or may be special providences and dispensations, as our fathers believed, by which we may escape this or that evil, but our good fortune is that we have our part and lot in the total scheme of things, that we share in the slow optimistic tendency of the universe, that we have life and health and wholeness on the same terms as the trees, the flowers, the grass, the animals have, and pay the same price for our well being, in struggle and effort, that they pay. That is our good fortune. There is nothing accidental or exceptional about it. It is not by the favor or disfavor of some god that things go well or ill with us, but it is by the authority of the whole universe, by the consent and coöperation of every force above us and beneath us. The natural forces crush and destroy man when he transgresses them, as they destroy or neutralize one another. He is a part of the system of things, and has a stake in every wind that blows and cloud that sails. It is to his final interest, whether he sees it or not, that water should always do the work of water, and fire do the work of fire, and frost do the work of frost, and gravity do the work of gravity, though they destroy him ("Though he slay me, yet will I trust him"), rather than that they should ever fail. In fact, he has his life and keeps it only because the natural forces and elements are always true to themselves, and are no respecters of persons.

We should not be here blustering around and sitting in judgment upon the ways of the Eternal, had not the ways of the Eternal been without variableness, or shadow of turning. If we or our fortunes go down prematurely beneath the currents, it is because the currents are vital, and do never and can never cease nor turn aside. The weakest force must give way, and the rotten timber break before the sound. We may fancy that there might be a better universe, but we cannot conceive of a better because our minds are the outcome of things as they are, and all our ideas of value are based upon the lessons we learn in this world.

Nature is as regardless of a planet or a sun as of a bubble upon the river, has one no more at heart than the other. How many suns have gone out? How many planets have perished? If the earth should collide with some heavenly body today and all its life be extinguished, would it not be just like spendthrift Nature? She has infinite worlds left, and out of old she makes new. You cannot lose or destroy heat or force, nor add to them, though you seem to do so. Nature wins in every game because she bets on both sides. If her suns or systems fail, it is, after all, her laws that succeed. A burnt-out sun vindicates the constancy of her forces.

As individuals we suffer defeat, injustice, pain, sorrow, premature death; multitudes perish to fertilize the soil that is to grow the bread of other multitudes; thousands but make a bridge of their dead bodies over which other thousands are to pass safely to some land of promise. The feeble, the idiotic, the deformed, seem to suffer injustice at the hands of their maker; there is no redress, no court of appeal for them; the verdict of natural law cannot be reversed. When the current of life shrinks in its channel, there are causes for it, and if these causes ceased to operate, the universe would go to pieces; but the individual whose measure, by reason of these causes, is only half full pays the price of the sins or the shortcomings of others; his misfortune but vindicates the law upon which our lives are all strung as beads upon a thread.

In an orchard of apple trees some of the fruit is wormy, some scabbed, some dwarfed, from one cause and another; but Nature approves of the worm, and of the fungus that makes the scab, and of the aphid that makes the dwarf, just as sincerely as she approves of the perfect fruit. She holds the stakes of both sides; she wins, whoever loses. An insect stings a leaf or a stem, and instantly all the forces and fluids that were building the leaf turn to building a home for the young of the insect; the leaf is forgotten, and only the needs of the insect remembered, and we thus have the oak gall and the hickory gall and other like abnormalities. The

247

cancer that is slowly eating a man up — it too is the result of a vital process just as much as is the life it is destroying. Contagion, infection, pestilence, illustrate the laws of life. One thing devours or destroys another — the parasite destroys its host, the rust destroys the wheat or the oats, the vermin destroy the poultry, and so forth; still the game of life goes on, and the best wins, if not to-day, then to-morrow, or in ten thousand years. In the meantime, struggle, pain, defeat, death, come in; we suffer, we sorrow, we appeal to the gods. But the gods smile and keep aloof, and the world goes blundering on because there are no other conditions of progress. Evil follows good as its shadow; it is inseparable from the constitution of things. It shades the picture, it affords the contrast, it gives the impetus. The good, the better, the best — these are defined to us, and made to entice us by their opposites. We never fully attain them because our standards rise as we rise; what satisfied us yesterday will not satisfy us to-day. Peace, satisfaction, true repose, come only through effort, and then not for long. I love to recall Whitman's words, and to think how true they are both for nations and for individuals : —

> "Now understand me well —
> It is provided in the essence of things, that from any fruition of success, no matter what, shall come forth something to make a greater struggle necessary."

II

Life means such different things to different men and to different generations of men; its values shift from age to age and from country to country. Think what it meant to our Puritan forefathers, the early settlers of New England — freedom of religious opinion, and to worship God in their own way. This was the paramount interest and value of life. To secure this, they were ready to make any sacrifice — friends, home, property, country — and to brave hardship and dangers to the end of their lives. In those days the religious idea pressed heavily upon the minds of men, and the main concern of life related to the other world. We in our time can hardly realize the absolute tyranny of religious prepossessions that the minds of our fathers were under, and that the minds of men were under through all the Middle Ages.

Huxley in his old age said: "It is a great many years since at the outset of my career I had to think seriously what life had to offer that was worth having. I came to the conclusion that the chief good for me was freedom to learn, think, and say what I pleased, when I pleased." This was the old Puritan spirit cropping out again, in quite a different field, and concerned with the truth as it is related to this world, quite irrespective of its possible bearing upon the next.

The value of life to Huxley lay in the opportunity to give free play to that truth-loving mind of his, no matter where the quest led him. If it led him into battle, as it was bound to do, so much the better. He was "ever a fighter." The love of Truth was his paramount passion, but he loved her all the more if he saw her life jeopardized and he could make a gallant charge for her rescue.

To have a mind eager to know the great truths and broad enough to take them in, and not get lost in the maze of apparent contradictions, is undoubtedly the highest good. This, I take it, is what our fathers meant in their way by saying the chief end of man was to serve God and glorify him forever. This formula is not suited to the temper of the modern scientific mind because of the theological savor that clings to it. Theological values have shrunken enormously in our time; but let the modern mind express the idea in its own terms, and it fully agrees. To love the Truth and possess it forever is the supreme good.

Of course Pilate's question of old comes up, What is truth? since one man's truth may be another man's falsehood. But not in the scientific realm, in the realm of verifiable objective truth. What is one man's truth here must be all men's truth. What is one man's truth in the business affairs of life — in trade, in banking, in mechanics, in agriculture, in law — must be all men's truth. It would seem as if what is one man's truth in so vital a matter as religion ought to be all men's truth. But it is not. Religion is such an intensely personal and subjective matter that no two men stand at just the same angle with reference to any one proposition, at least to the evidence of the truth of that proposition. The question of the soul's immortality seems such a vital question to some, while others are quite indifferent to it. One man says, I must have proof. I cannot rest in the idea that death ends all. Another says, What matters it? I am not sure I want endless existence. Ingersoll felt this way. Then if death does end all, we shall not lie in our graves lamenting our fate. If it does not, so much the better.

But is any form of religious belief such a vital matter after all? What noble and beautiful lives have been lived by people of just opposite religious creeds. A man's creed, in our day at least, seems to affect his life little more than the clothes he wears. The church has lost its power, its promises have lost their lure, its threats have lost their terror. It is a question why church attendance has so fallen off. In earlier times people attended church from a sense of duty; now the masses go only when there is a promise of pleasure, and that is less and less often.

Errors of religious belief are not serious. If they were, chaos would have come long ago. Each age repudiates or modifies the creed of the preceding, trims it or renews it as a man trims his orchard, lopping off the dead branches, or grafting new ones on, or resetting it entirely. All denominations are grafting on more liberal and more charitable views. The stock of religious ideas is undoubtedly improving — less personal, perhaps, but more broadly intellectual — generalizations from more universal facts.

In morality, what is one man's truth ought to be all men's truth, because morality is a matter of conduct toward our fellows. We may fail to keep our promises to our gods and nothing comes of it, but if we forget our promissory notes, something does come of it, and, as like as not, that something takes the form of the sheriff.

The scientific mind, like Huxley's, looks with amazement upon the credulity of the theological mind, upon its low standard of evidence.

There are currents and currents in life. A river is one kind of current, the Gulf Stream is another. The currents in the affairs of men are more like the latter — obscure in their origin, vague and shifting in their boundaries, and mysterious in their endings, and the result of large cosmic forces. There are movements in the history of men's minds that are local and temporary like that, say, of the Crusaders, or of Witchcraft, and there are others that are like ocean currents, a trend of the universal mind. The rise and growth of rationalism seems of this kind.

the scientific spirit, the desire to prove all things, and to hold fast to that which is good. It is the conditions of proof that have become strenuous and exacting. The standard of the good has not gone up so much as the standard of evidence. We prove a thing now not by an appeal to a text of some book, or to any ecclesiastical court, but by an appeal to reason. An appeal to conscience is not conclusive, because conscience is more or less the creature of the hour, or of custom, or of training, but reason emancipates us from all false or secondary considerations, and enables us to see the thing as it is, in and of itself.

III

I have drifted into deeper waters than I intended to when I set out. I meant to have kept nearer the shore. I have had, I say, a happy life. When I was a young man (twenty-five), I wrote a little poem called "Waiting," which has had quite a history, and the burden of which is, "My own shall come to me." What my constitution demands, the friends, the helps, the fulfillments, the opportunities, I shall find somewhere, some time. It was a statement of the old doctrine of the elective affinities. Those who are born to strife and contention find strife and contention ready at their hand; those who are born for gentleness and love find gentleness and love drawn to them. The naturally suspicious and distrustful find the world in conspiracy against them; the unkind, the hard-hearted, see themselves in their fellows about them. The tone in which we speak to the world, the world speaks to us. Give your best and you will get the best in return. Give in heaping measure and in heaping measure it shall be returned. We all get our due sooner or later, in one form or another. "Be not weary in well doing;" the reward will surely come, if not in worldly goods, then in inward satisfaction, grace of spirit, peace of mind.

All the best things of my life have come to me unsought, but I hope not unearned. That would contradict the principle of equity I have been illustrating. A man does not, in the long run, get wages he has not earned. What I mean is that most of the good things of my life — friends, travel, opportunity — have been unexpected. I do not feel that fortune has driven sharp bargains with me. I am not a disappointed man. Blessed is he who expects little, but works as if he expected much. Sufficient unto the day is the *good* thereof. I have invested myself in the present moment, in the things near at hand, in the things that all may have on equal terms. If one sets one's heart on the exceptional, the far-off — on riches, on fame, on power — the chances are he will be disappointed; he will waste his time seeking a short cut to these things. There is no short cut. For anything worth having one must pay the price, and the price is always work, patience, love, self-sacrifice — no paper currency, no promises to pay, but the gold of real service.

I am not decrying ambition, the aiming high, only there is no use aiming unless you are loaded, and it is the loading, and the kind of material to be used, that one is first to be solicitous about.

"Serene I fold my hands and wait;" but if I have waited one day, I have hustled the next. If I have had faith that my own would come to me, I have tried to make sure that it was my own, and not that of another. Waiting with me has been mainly a cheerful acquiescence in the order of the universe as I found it — a faith in the essential veracity of things. I have waited for the sun to rise and for the seasons to come; I have waited for a chance to put in my oar. Which way do the currents of my being set? What do I love that is worthy and of good report? I will extend myself in this direction; I will annex this territory. I will not wait to see if this or that pays, if this or that notion draws the multitude. I will wait only till I can see my way clearly. In the meantime I will be clearing my eyes and training them to know the real values of life when they see them.

Waiting for some one else to do your work, for what you have not earned to come to you, is to murder time. Waiting for something to turn up is equally poor policy, unless you have already set the currents going that will cause a particular something to turn up. The farmer waits for his harvest after he has sown the seed. The sailor waits for a breeze after he has spread his sail. Much of life is taken up in waiting — fruitful waiting.

I never have sought wealth, I have been too much absorbed in enjoying the world about me. I had no talent for business anyhow — for the cutthroat competition that modern business for the most part is — and probably could not have attained wealth had I desired it. I dare not aver that I had really rather be cheated than to cheat, but I am quite sure I could never knowingly overreach a man, and what chance of success could such a tenderfoot have in the conscienceless struggle for money that goes on in the business world? I am a fairly successful farmer and fruit-grower. I love the soil, I love to see the crops grow and mature, but the marketing of them, the turning of them into money, grinds my soul because of the sense of strife and competition that pervades the air of the market-place. If one could afford to give one's fruit away, after he had grown it to perfection, to people who would be sure to appreciate it, that would be worth while, and would leave no wounds. But that is what I have in a sense done with my intellectual products. I have not written one book for money (yes, one, and that was a failure); I have written them for love, and the modest sum they have brought me has left no sting.

AN OUTLOOK UPON LIFE

I look upon this craze for wealth that possesses nearly all classes in our time as one of the most lamentable spectacles the world has ever seen. The old prayer, "Give me neither poverty nor riches," is the only sane one. The grand mistake we make is in supposing that because a little money is a good thing, unlimited means is the sum of all good, or that our happiness will keep pace with the increase of our possessions. But such is not the case, because the number of things we can really make our own is limited. We cannot drink the ocean be we ever so thirsty. A cup of water from the spring is all we need. A friend of mine once said that if he outlived his wife, he should put upon her tombstone, "Died of Things" — killed by the multitude of her possessions. The number of people who are thus killed is no doubt very great. When Thoreau found that the specimens and curiosities that had accumulated upon his mantel-piece needed dusting, he pitched them out of the window.

The massing of a great fortune is a perilous enterprise. The giving away of a great fortune is equally a perilous enterprise, not to the man who gives it — it ought to be salutary to him — but to his beneficiaries.

Very many of the great fortunes of our time have been accumulated by a process like that of turning all the streams into your private reservoir: they have caused a great many people somewhere to be short of water, and have taken away the power of many busy, peaceful wheels. The ideal condition is an even distribution of wealth. When you try to give away your monstrous fortune, to open your dam, then danger begins, because you cannot return the waters to their natural channels. You must make new channels, and you may do more harm than good. It never can go now where it would have gone. The wealth is in a measure redistributed, without enriching those from whom it originally came. Few millionaires could face the questions: Have you rendered a service to your fellows in proportion to your wealth? Have you earned your fortune, or have you grabbed it? Is it an addition to the wealth of the world, or a subtraction from the wealth which others have earned? The wealth that comes to a man through his efforts in furthering the work of the world and promoting the good of all is the only worthy wealth.

Beyond the point of a moderate competency, wealth is a burden. A man may possess a competency; great wealth possesses him. He is the victim. It fills him with unrest; it destroys or perverts his natural relations to his fellows; it corrupts his simplicity; it thrusts the false values of life before him; it gives him power which it is dangerous to exercise; it leads to self-indulgence; it hardens the heart; it fosters a false pride. To give it away is perilous; to keep it is to invite care and vexation of spirit. For a rich man to lead the simple life is about as hard as for a camel to go through the needle's eye. How many things stand between him and the simple open air of our common humanity! Marcus Aurelius thought a man might be happy even in a palace; but it takes a Marcus Aurelius — a man whose simplicity of character is incorruptible — to be so. Yet I have no disposition to rail at wealth as such, though the penalties and dangers that attend it are very obvious. I never expect to see it go out of fashion. Its unequal distribution in all times, no doubt, results from natural causes.

Sooner or later things find their proper level, and the proper level of some things is on top. In the jostle and strife of this world the strong men, the master minds, are bound to be on top. This is inevitable; the very laws of matter are on their side.

Not socialism, or any other "ism," can permanently equalize the fortunes of men. The strong will dominate, the weak must succumb. "For whosoever hath, to him shall be given, and he shall have more abundance: but whosoever hath not, from him shall be taken away even that he hath." Power draws power; inefficiency loses even that which it hath. To abolish poverty, to abolish wealth, we must first abolish the natural inequality among mankind. It is as if some men had longer arms than others and could reach the fruit on the tree of opportunity beyond the grasp of their competitors. Shall we cut off their arms? No, we can only shame them out of making hogs of themselves and of laying up greater stores than they can possibly use. In our day and country, the golden fruit on the tree has been so abundant that the long-armed men have degenerated into wealth-maniacs, and have resorted to all manner of unfair means; they have trampled down the shorter-armed men, and gained an advantage on their prostrate bodies. That is where the injustice comes in. Some of our monstrous trusts and combines, for instance, have killed competition by foul and underhanded means; they have crowded or thrust their competitors entirely away from the tree, or else have mounted up on their shoulders. They have resorted to the methods of the robber and assassin.

I am bound to praise the simple life, because I have lived it and found it good. When I depart from it, evil results follow. I love a small house, plain clothes, simple living. Many persons know the luxury of a skin bath — a plunge in the pool or the wave unhampered by clothing. That is the simple life — direct and immediate contact with things, life with the false wrappings torn away — the fine house, the fine equipage, the expensive habits, all cut off. How free one feels, how good the elements taste, how close one gets to them, how they fit one's body and one's soul! To see the fire that warms you, or better yet, to cut the wood that feeds the fire that warms you; to see the spring where the water bubbles up that slakes your thirst, and to dip your pail into it; to see the beams that are the stay of your four walls, and the timbers that uphold the roof that shelters you; to be in direct and personal contact with the sources of your material life; to want no extras, no shields; to find the universal elements enough; to find the air and the water exhilarating; to be refreshed by a morning walk or an evening saunter; to find a quest of wild berries more satisfying than a gift of tropic fruit; to be thrilled by the stars at night; to be elated over a bird's nest, or over a wild flower in spring — these are some of the rewards of the simple life.

XIII

"ALL'S RIGHT WITH THE WORLD"

I

WHETHER or not we can accept Browning's morning line, "All's right with the world," depends upon our point of view. To the intellect, the disinterested faculties, undoubtedly, all's right with the world. To the seeing mind nature presents a series, an infinite series, of logical sequences; cause and effect are inseparably joined, and things could in no wise be other than what they are. The forces that destroy us are only going their appointed ways, and if they turned out or made an exception on our account, the very foundations of the universe would be impeached.

The creation is good, and man's explanation and vindication of it have given rise to what we call science. One recalls Whitman's lines: —

"I lie abstracted and hear beautiful tales of things and the reasons of things,
They are so beautiful I nudge myself to listen."

To our æsthetic faculties, all's right with the world. What beauty, what grandeur, what perfection! the sum of all we know or can know of these qualities. Sin, decay, ruin, death — all add to the picturesqueness of the world.

But to our moral sentiments, our sense of goodness, mercy, justice, benevolence, humility, self-denial — all those tender and restraining feelings that are called into action through our relations to our fellows, all is not right with the world. All, or nearly all, is wrong with the world. So much so that our fathers, to account for it, had to suppose some dire catastrophe had befallen creation and frustrated the original plan of the Creator. Hence the myth of Adam and Eve in the Garden, and the forbidden fruit that

"Brought death into the world and all our woe."

The world is full of pain, suffering, cruelty, sin, defeat, injustice, hope deferred, calamities of fire, flood, storm, pestilence, wars, famine — young lives cut off in their bloom, old lives ending in sorrow and decrepitude, iniquity on the throne, virtue in the dust. How is love thwarted, how is pity shocked, how is our sense of mercy and of justice outraged, when we look out upon the world, past or present!

Tract after tract of history is knee-deep with blood, and mostly innocent blood. The cruelty of rulers, the blindness and infatuation of the people, the superstition of priests — waste, failures, anguish, treachery, greed everywhere — how the moral nature revolts at the spectacle of it all!

Cardinal Newman drew back from the spectacle with the deepest distress. Not seeing God in the world, he said, was like looking into a mirror and not seeing his own face there. He could account for the fact only by inferring that the human race was implicated in some terrible aboriginal calamity. Had the cardinal looked creation over, he would have seen evidence of the same merciless strife, the same cruel struggle, and mystery, and failure everywhere.

This is the verdict of the moral sense, the cry of the wounded heart. It is not the vision of the intellect, it is the plaint of the benevolent emotions. In the face of it all the serene reason still sings, All 's well with the world, all 's well with man; still he mounts and mounts; " rise after rise bow the phantoms behind " him; sin and suffering are a condition of growth and development; the great laws are impersonal; the God of the intellect is without variableness or shadow of turning, he sends his rain upon the just and the unjust alike, and though he slay me, yet will I trust him; though a cry of pain and anguish ever goes up from the earth to a deaf heaven, the reason sees that life and the joy of life can be had on no other terms.

Newman found God only when he looked into his own conscience, into that artificial personality, as Huxley called it, which has been built up in each of us through ages of contact with our fellows,

There he found the benevolence, the love, the sense of justice, which he failed to find in the world without. It is not a mere fling or witty retort that man creates God in his own image; it is profoundly true. And then he torments himself that he does not see this image reflected in nature. More and more, as his evolution goes on, he loves mercy, justice, goodness, and more and more he endows his gods with these attributes. In the long-past time, when those sentiments were far less developed in man, we find his gods much more cruel and wicked.

All moral and ethical sentiments and aspirations are purely personal, and relate to man in society. They are the fruit of the social aggregate. It may be said with a measure of truth that while man's intellect is from God, his moral nature is the work of his own hands. His reason is reflected in the course of nature; it is in unison with the cosmic process; it looks upon the world and says it is good; it is consistent and fulfills its own end. But his moral nature is not reflected in the objective world; there is hardly a trace of it there; there is only law which knows no mercy, or tenderness, or forgiveness, or self-sacrifice, and which is oblivious to pain and suffering. Hence the God which our moral nature demands is not found in the world; to the cosmic process he is a stranger; it rules him out as it rules out all our human weaknesses. Fly to the uttermost parts of the earth, and you will not find him there, or soar to the heavens or dive to the depths, and you will not find him there. Infinite and eternal power you find, but not the God of love and mercy that the moral nature craves. Only in the human heart do you find this God. Hence our fathers looked upon man as something entirely apart from nature; he was not the result of the cosmic process, but a special creation, endowed with special powers, and given an immortal soul, which was denied to all other creatures.

It is only by regarding man as a part of nature, as the outcome of the same vital forces underfoot and overhead that the plants and the animals are, that we can find God in the world.

When the intellect from its height of observation surveys man and the world, it sees that he is necessarily a part of nature, and that all he has done and thought and suffered, all his arts and religions and literatures, all his dreams and visions and aspirations, came out of the earth, were evolved through the working of natural or cosmic laws, because the reasoning mind cannot admit of the arbitrary introduction of any force or influence from without. The chain of cause and effect is never broken, and all the noble and godlike traits of man, all his love and heroism and self-denial, as well as all his baser animal traits — his hates, his revenges, his cruelty, his lusts, his meannesses of one kind or another — are not from some extraneous source, are not fortuitous and unrelated, but have their root in the constitution of things. There is nothing on or in the earth that is not of the earth; it is all latent or patent in the cosmic process.

II

Strange how men have speculated about the origin of evil, and built themselves cages in which to bruise their own wings. Evil has been regarded as something as positive as light, or heat, or any tangible object. Our moral and religious nature has so regarded it, but the reason sees that evil is only the shadow of good, and is as inevitable as good is inevitable. Life has its positive and its negative sides. Its positive side is health and growth and enjoyment, its negative side is disease and decay and suffering. All that favors the former is good, all that leads to the latter is bad, relatively bad. Disease is only another form of life. The germs that are pulling us down and destroying us in typhoid fever or cholera are healthy and thriving if we are not. What is good for them is bad for us. Life preys upon life everywhere, and the devoured is the victim of evil. We live and move and have our being submerged in an ocean of germs, myriads of them for us and myriads of them against us on occasion; one kind building up, another kind pulling down, and, as it were, redistributing the type. Life as we know it could not go on without both kinds. Without the germs of fermentation, for instance, what would happen to the world? Without the germs that break down animal and vegetable tissue and redistribute the elements of which they are composed — the germs of death — how long could life go on?

A fever tortures and burns my flesh because the body fights against the germs that would destroy it. It is one form of life struggling with another form. A festering pool in the fields or woods conceals chemical processes that all favor life.

Life is the result of a certain balance between what we call good and evil forces. Destroy that balance, that harmonious adjustment, and death or disease follows. We imperil it when we eat too much, or drink too much, or work too hard, or sleep too little, or exclude the air and sunlight from our houses. A pestilence is just as much an evidence of the health and soundness of nature as is immunity from it, only it is the health of forces that for reasons antagonize our health. We have let the enemy encamp and intrench in our midst while we slumbered. If we had life on easier terms than eternal vigilance, what would it be worth? If we want to escape blow-flies and mosquitoes and the contagion of this or that, let us go to the Arctic or Antarctic regions, where death reigns perpetual.

Struggle is the condition of evolution, and evolution is the road all life has traveled. Moral evil pertains only to man, and is incident to his growth and development. To bear false witness against one's neighbor, or to steal, or to be cruel or covetous, are moral evils which we become conscious of only when we have reached a higher moral plane. The animal is not involved in such evils. Violence and fraud and injustice attest the existence of higher qualities. They are shadows and not real entities, the shortcomings of the unripe animal man. A foul day is just as much a legitimate part of our weather system as a fair day; and is it in itself any more evil?

What I mean to say is that the whole category of moral evils, from petty slander to gigantic stealing, from political corruption to social debauchery, are only eddies or back currents that attest the onward flow of moral progress. A parasite is an evil, but it could not exist without a host to prey upon.

Moral evil, like physical evil, is bestowed by the same hand that bestows the moral good; it is the fruit of the same tree — the wormy and scabby fruit — and while every effort is to be made to remedy it, we are not to regard it as something foreign to us, something the origin of which is involved in mystery, a subject for metaphysical or theological hair-splitting, and adequate to account for the strained relations, as our fathers viewed it, between God and man. Development implies imperfection; as long as our course is upward, we have

270

not yet reached the top of the hill. Our standards
rise as we rise, and the ideal always does and always
will outrun the real. We may produce a perfect
apple or a perfect peach, or plum, or pear, but not
a perfect man, because to man are opened infinite
possibilities. Perfect in honesty, in sobriety, in
truthfulness, but not perfect in love, or sympathy,
in self-denial, in veneration, or in wisdom. That
good and evil are not such strangers is seen in the
fact that present evil may turn out a future good,
and *vice versa*. All the world looks upon poverty
as an evil, yet of what men has it been the making!
Reverses in business have often put a man upon a
road that led to a higher success than was possible
under the old conditions, a success which only veri-
fies the soundness of the principles the disregarding
of which led to the past failure. If gravity did not
pull your faulty structure down, it would not enable
your sound structure to stand up. If the rain did
not come through your rotten roof, it would not
percolate to the roots of the grass in the ground.
Indeed, to abolish the possibility of evil from the
universe would be to abolish the possibility of good.
If vice and crime did not arise under certain conditions in society, all social progress would be barred.
Out of the desire to better our condition comes the
greed of wealth and the hoggishness of the million-
aire. Out of sex love comes lust and fornication;
out of the instinct of self-preservation comes base

selfishness; the feeling of self-respect pushed a little too far becomes pride and vainglory; faith degenerates into credulity, worship into idolatry, deference into fawning, firmness into hardness of heart, self-reliance into arrogance. The danger that threatens repose is stagnation, that threatens industry is greed, that threatens thrift is avarice, that threatens power is tyranny. Everywhere are things linked together, every virtue has its vice, every good has its ill, every sweet has its bitter, and the bitter is often the best medicine.

What shall we say, then? Shall we be tolerant of evil? Shall we embrace vice as well as virtue? No; but we shall cease to try to persuade ourselves "that the celestial laws need to be worked over and rectified," that there is some ingrained defect in God's universe, and that the divine plan miscarried; that man in this world has got the bad end of a bad bargain. We get sooner or later what we pay for, and we do not get what we do not pay for, and there is no credit system.

"All's right with the world." I know it does not soothe the bruises of the victim of a railroad smash-up to be told that the laws of force could not act differently, nor the disappointment of the farmer when his crops are burned up by the drought to be assured that the weather system is still running all right elsewhere, nor the sick and the suffering to be told that pain too is a guardian angel; and yet it

is something to know that things look better under
the surface, that there is no profound conspiracy
of evil against us, that the universe really has the
well-being of each of us at heart, and that if we fall
short of that well-being, we are not the victims of a
malignant spirit, but the sufferers from the operation of a beneficent law.

The universe has our well-being at heart in a
general, universal sense, and not in a personal sense.
For instance, our lives depend upon the bounty of
the rain, and yet the rain does not accommodate
itself to the special personal needs of this man or
that man, and it may result in a flood that brings
death and ruin in its path. Like all other things in
nature, it is a general beneficence to which we have
to accommodate ourselves. It rains alike upon the
just and the unjust, upon the sea and upon the
land, upon the sown field and upon the mown hay
— a broadcast, wholesale kind of providence.

I confess that from the course of life and the processes of nature one cannot infer the existence of
a Being such as our fathers worshiped — a kind of
omnipresent man, whose relation to the universe
was that of maker and governor.

We get instead the conception of an infinite
power, not separable from the universe, but one
with it, as the soul is one with the body, which
finally expresses itself in man as reason, as love, as
awe, as beauty, as aspiration, as righteousness; in

the brute world as instinct, cunning, ferocity, and other animal traits; in the material world as law, system, development, power. When we think of God in any kind of human relation to the universe, or as a being apart from it, as parent, judge, sovereign, guide, we at once stumble upon this problem of evil, and invent schemes to justify God's ways to man, to excuse or gloss over the cruelty, the suffering, the injustice, we see in the world; we invent the devil, the garden of Eden, the myth of the fall of man, sin, the atonement, the judgment day. These things flow naturally from our anthropomorphic conception of God. They help reconcile the irreconcilable; they bridge over the chasm. But to the naturalistic conception, as distinguished from the theological, these things are childish dreams, to be put from us as we put away other childish things. Sin has no more reality than the negative gravity that Frank Stockton imagined, redemption no more reality than the rebellion in heaven that Milton invented, and heaven and hell no more existence than any other fabled abode of the ancient world.

To science, every day is a judgment day, eternity is now and here, heaven lies all about us, all laws are celestial laws. God is literally in everything we see and hear and feel, in every flower that blows, and not a sparrow falls to the ground without his cognizance. Your days are appointed, and all the hairs of your head are numbered, because nothing goes by chance in this universe. Not a snowflake falls but its form and its course are determined by forces as old as the universe; pitch a stone from your hand and the elder gods know exactly where it shall alight. Is not this good predestinarianism? Yes, but not as Jonathan Edwards saw it; it is as science sees it. It is good everlastingism — the ways of a Power without variableness or shadow of turning, which Edwards anthropomorphized into a cruel, despotic, almighty man. We are predestined to heaven or hell by the dispositions we inherit from our fathers, by the environment which society makes for us, by the age and country in which we live, and by the strength and weakness of our own characters, which again are the result of forces as old as the race, and as constant and impersonal in their activity as gravitation.

The rising vapor proves gravitation as fully as the falling rain. The wildest, freest thing on wings goes only its appointed way. With the course of the swallow hawking for insects in the air, or with the course of the insects themselves soaring in the sunshine, the hand of chance plays no part any more than it does with the sailboat obeying wind and current on yonder bay, which again is a good symbol of a man's course throughout this world, impelled by impulses inherited from his fathers, and awakened by the circumstances of his life.

We speak of the chance meeting of this man and

275

that woman which resulted in a union for life, and, so far as their conscious wills were concerned, the meeting was a matter of chance; but if we could see all the forces that have been at work to bring them together, we should discover that there was no more chance about it than about the conjunction of two planets in the evening sky.

Indeed, our lives are evidently the result of such a play and interplay of forces from far and from near, from the past and from the present, from the earth and from the heavens, forces so subtle and constant and so beyond the reach of our analysis, that one is half converted to the claims of astrology, and inclined to believe that the fate of each of us was written in the heavens before the foundations of the world.

III

Don't you suppose that if the trees in the forest, the grass in the field, the fruit in the orchard, could for a moment be conscious and speak, they would each and all say, There is evil here also, there is crime, there is sin, there is struggle, defeat, and death also? One plant could complain that there is another plant stealing from it, or trespassing upon its territory and robbing it; another is being crowded to the wall, another being dwarfed by its bigger and more sturdy neighbor. Cut down a tree in the forest, and in the spring a half dozen or more shoots start from the stump to replace the parent trunk. They all grow vigorously the first season; the whole push of the complex root system of the stump is behind them. They grow vigorously the second season, and the third, and maybe for several years more. But the competition becomes sharper and sharper; some of the shoots, from causes hard to penetrate, outstrip their fellows, they get the lead, they get more light, more foliage, and this enables them to take up more nourishment from the soil. The others lag, then stop, then die. Then the struggle among the three or four or five thrifty shoots goes on for a few years longer, till some of them are distanced, and finally die when they are the size of one's leg. Then two or three remain to take the place of the parent trunk. We witness here the same struggle that we witness in the animal world. It is all a question of the means of subsistence; the soil can nourish only just so much life, and the fittest or luckiest gets this nourishment, just the same as when you throw a bone to a pack of hungry dogs.

Sometimes the grain will "run out" the weeds, and sometimes the weeds will run out the grain, or the grass. The cereals that depend upon man, and that he depends upon, cannot of course hold their own with the wild denizens of the soil. Much care and culture has made them weak; they have grown dependent; they must be fed and cosseted and protected, the battle against the foes of life

277

must be fought for them. All these cultivated plants are handicapped by a burden the wild things do not bear; the wild things are mainly bent only upon self-propagation: to this end their seeds are small and numerous; but the cultivated grains and vegetables bear a burden of food for man, aside from the germ necessary to their propagation. Wild rice is a lean, savage, hirsute product compared with the cultivated varieties; but the potato and the onion and the pippin — what a burden of starch and of other elements each bears, in contrast with the wild species!

Evil comes to the fruit tree in the orchard in the shape of frost that nips the fruit buds, or of worms that eat its foliage, or in the shape of birds that cut out the heart of the blossom, or in the shape of insects that lay their eggs in the baby fruit, or in the shape of fungus growths that fasten upon it and dwarf it or mar it. Evil threatens and sooner or later comes to everything that lives. Evil in this sense is a necessary part of the living universe; there is no escape from it. A world of competition, of diverse and opposed interests, is a world of struggle, of defeat, of death.

After the ice has been all nicely formed in the river, a miracle of crystallic beauty and perfection, the winds or the tides break it up and bring chaos to it. But the cold continues, the ice-packs freeze together, or new ice forms, the ruin of the first venture of the frost is a stepping-stone in the second; the river is again covered and may be again broken up, but by and by, under a still lower temperature, the thing is done and the river permanently frozen over. Then the struggle is between the frost and the sun till, in the spring, the latter wins.

IV

At least one thing is certain as the result of man's sojourn on this planet: he is becoming more and more at home on it, more and more on good terms with the nature around him. His childish fear and dread of it is largely gone. He now makes playfellows of things which once filled him with terror; he makes servants of forces that he once thought stood ready to devour him; he is in partnership with the sun and moon and all the hosts of heaven. He no longer peoples the air and the earth with evil spirits. The darkness of the night, or of caverns and forests, no longer conceals malignant powers or influences that are lying in wait to devour him. Even Milton speaks of

"this drear wood,
The nodding horror of whose shady brows
Threats the forlorn and wandering passenger."

To us the wood is filled with beauty and interest; the mountain is a challenge to climb to a vaster and higher outlook, and the abysmal seas hold records we would fain recover and peruse. Evil omens and prognostications have disappeared. Dread of Nature has been followed by curiosity about Nature, and curiosity has been followed by love. Men now love Nature as I fancy they have never loved her before. I fancy also that we have come to realize as never before the truth of the Creator's verdict upon his work: "And behold it was good."

To what do we owe this change? To the growth of the human reason led and fostered by science. Science has showed man that he is not an alien in the universe, that he is not an interloper, that he is not an exile from another sphere, or arbitrarily put here, but that he is the product of the forces that surround him. Science has banished the arbitrary, the miraculous, the exceptional, from nature, and instead of these things has revealed order, system, and the irrefragable logic of cause and effect. Instead of good and bad spirits contending with one another, it reveals an inevitable beneficence and a steady upward progress. It shows that the universe is made of one stuff, and that no atom can go amiss or lose its way.

When we look at man and his goings and comings at a far enough remove, I think we surely see that he is under laws and influences that he knows not of. In the Orient he shows one set of influences, in the Occident another. In the south he is of one temper, in the north of another. The stamp of his environment, of his climate, is upon him. Born in one age, he is seized with the spirit of adventure and plants colonies and kingdoms. Born in another, he rusts out at home. One age is of one complexion, another of another; one is an age of faith, the next an age of skepticism; the enthusiasm of one age is the joke of the next. We are puppets all, and obey unseen masters. The Time-spirit sets its seal upon us. The electric currents or the waves of vibration that cause the steel filings to spring into patterns are like the influences in an age that cause men to form parties and groups of one kind or another, swayed by a common impulse, the origin of which is in the will of none of them.

What, then, becomes of the freedom of the will of which we are all conscious? We do as we like. Yes, but what determines our liking? In this freedom fate is deftly concealed. Our choice is along the lines of forces or inborn tendencies of which we are unconscious. We are free to do as our inherited traits, our temperament, our environment, our training, the influence of the climate over us, and the geography and geology about us and beneath us decide. But these things are vital in us, and therefore we are unconscious of them. Hence our sense of free choice is not obstructed; we still do as we like, only something beyond our wills determines what we shall like.

The intellectual nature of man was developed long before his moral nature. His sense of beauty, of art, of ornament, is older than his sense of justice or mercy. Indeed, he was a religious being before he was a moral being. He worshiped and offered sacrifices before he dealt justly and humanely with his fellow.

Unless what we mean by good prevailed over the bad, we should not be here. If some sort of order and peace had not come out of the primal warring of the elements, man could not have appeared. The waters have been gathered together, the continents have been lifted up, the vapors have learned to form clouds, the soil has been formed, and the benediction of the flowers and of the grass is upon the hills. The destructive elemental forces have subsided. In nearly all parts of the earth man can subsist. The benevolence of Providence is seen in this general, inevitable course of nature. Right actions meet with their reward; health and wholeness are possible; deal fairly and squarely with Nature, and you always get the worth of your money. We know the conditions of disease; we know the conditions of health. The ways of the Eternal are appointed, and we may find them out.

Truly to obey the will of God is our salvation, but we must look for this will, not in some book or creed, but in the order of the universe, in the sequence of cause and effect.

INDEX

INDEX

INDEX

darkness on, 65; effect of domestication on, 68–70; gradation of, 71, 72; stamp of environment on, 78–84; influence of the male instinct of reproduction on, 87, 88, 91–100; influence of the gregarious instinct on, 87–91.

Coloration, protective, 51–100.

Columbine, 35.

Coon. See Raccoon.

Cows, path-making on hillsides by, 156, 157; a cow opening a gate, 157, 158; milk-manufacturing by, 159; a cow and a stuffed calf, 180.

Crabs, courtship of, 99.

Creeper, brown (*Certhia familiaris americana*), coloration and habits of, 86, 87.

Crow (*Corvus brachyrhynchos*), relation of coloration to habits of, 90; its manner of picking up food from water, 116, 117.

Cuckoo, 30.

Darwin, Charles, 65, 72; his theory of sexual selection, 92–100; reason and imagination in, 112; quoted on taste in birds, 151, 167; quoted on the casarita, 181, 182; Carlyle on, 215, 218.

Dogs, biting a stone, 131; anger in, 131; human traits in, 143–146; John Muir's dog, 149; Hobhouse's experiments with, 161; hunting woodchucks, 162; lack of reasoning in, 188, 189.

Ducks, 70, 71; a prodigal, 192, 193.

Dust, the substance of all things, 199.

Eagle, 117.

Eaton, Daniel Cady, 22.

Edwards, Jonathan, 275.

Electricity, 209.

Elephants, Hobhouse's experiments with, 160, 161.

Emerson, Ralph Waldo, quoted, 242.

Erythronium, or fawn lily, 185, 186.

Eternity, 238.

Eugénie, Empress, 6.

Evil, the origin of, 268–270; good impossible without, 270–272; no conspiracy of, 273; the universal struggle against, 276–279.

Evolution, 215–240.

Fabre, J. H., his experiments on a wasp and a bee, 184, 185.

Farm, the call of the, 36–38.

Farmer, the, and his fields, 45–50.

Fear, in wild and domestic animals, 69, 70.

Fields, the farmer's, 45–50.

Fire, origin of, 235.

Flamingo (*Phœnicopterus ruber*), 89.

Flicker. See High-hole.

Flycatcher, great crested (*Myiarchus crinitus*), 23.

Fox, 109, 114.

Fox, arctic, 57.

Freedom of will, 281.

Freeman, Edward Augustus, 110–112.

Frog, wood, 66.

Froude, James Anthony, 110–112.

Geddes, Patrick, and J. Arthur Thomson, their "Evolution of Sex," 100.

Geologic time, 236, 237.

Goat, mountain, 58.

God, the first cause, 228; the immanent, 233; Cardinal Newman's view of, 265; created by man in his image, 266; in the human heart, 266, 267; as seen in the universe, 273, 274; his will to be found in the order of the universe, 282.

Grasshoppers, colors of, 66.

Gregariousness, its influence on the colors of animals, 88–91; in man and animals, 135, 136.

Groos, Karl, 149.

Grosbeak, rose-breasted (*Zamelodia ludoviciana*), 32, 76.

Grouse, ruffed (*Bonasa umbellus*), coloration and feeding habits of, 87.

Hamerton, Philip Gilbert, his story of a cow, 180.

286

INDEX

Hare, northern, 63.
Heron, great blue (*Ardea herodias*),
  relation of coloration and habits
  of, 90.
High-hole, *or* flicker (*Colaptes
  auratus luteus*), 182.
Hobhouse, L. T., his "Mind and
  Evolution," 160–162.
Homing instinct, the, 126, 127.
Hornaday, William T., 177.
Hornet, black, 162.
Hornets, 197.
Huxley, Thomas Henry, 159, 163,
  190; and Carlyle, 215, 218, 224,
  237; a fighter, 250, 265; quoted,
  207, 208, 249.

Ichneumon-fly, 185.
Immortality, 251.
Infinite, the, 238–240.
Instinct, and reason, 177, 178; a
  kind of intelligence, 179; auto-
  matism of, 179–188; the response to, 189; the sufficiency
  of, 196, 198.

June, the opening of, 26–32.

Keller, Helen, 11.

Lemming, 64, 186, 187.
Life, first appearance of, 208; the
  origin of, 229–236; the mechan-
  ico-chemical theory of, 232–234;
  positive and negative sides of,
  268, 269; a balance between
  good and evil forces, 269.
Life (of man), meaning of, 241–261.
Lily, fawn. *See* Erythronium.
Long, William J., 198.
Loon (*Gavia imber*), 118.
Lost persons, tendency to turn in
  one direction, 20.
Love, sharpens the senses, 2; the
  measure of life, 3.
Lyell, Sir Charles, 218.

Maeterlinck, Maurice, 175.
Man, ancestry of, 215–224, 226–
  229, 236, 237; at home in the
  universe, 221; relationship with
  the -anthropoid apes, 222–224;
  a part of nature, 267; more and

more at home in the world, 279,
  280; development of the moral
  nature of, 281, 282.
Meadowlark (*Sturnella magna*),
  notes of, 35.
Mind, in matter, 212, 213.
Morality, truth in, 252.
Morgan, C. Lloyd, quoted on rea-
  son in animals, 178.
Morgan, L. H., 194.
Moth, expanding wings of a, 15,
  16; a yellowish-white, 17.
Moth, Cecropia, cocoon of, 19.
Moth, Promethea, cocoon of, 18.
Muir, John, 149.
Mushrooms, colors of, 67.

Natural history, truth and falsehood in, 101–115, 122, 123.
Nature, an inexhaustible storehouse, 3; demoralized by man,
  69; tendency to harmony in,
  79, 80; truth and falsehood in
  writing about, 101–115, 122,
  123; the school of, 197; a spendthrift, 246; wins in every game,
  246, 247.
Nature fakers, 101–115, 122, 123.
Newman, Cardinal, 265, 266.
Nuthatch, white-bellied (*Sitta caro-
  linensis*), colors and habits of, 86,
  87.

Observation, considered as an art,
  1, 2; love the secret of, 2, 3; difference between people in powers
  of, 4–10; training of powers of,
  11, 12; sharpened by the thought,
  21–23; power of accurate, possessed by few, 116, 118.
Observer, a close, 7–9.
Orchards, blossoming, 31, 32.
Oriole, puncturing grapes, 21.
Oriole, Baltimore (*Icterus galbula*),
  compared with orchard oriole,
  85; two pairs fighting, 191.
Oriole, orchard (*Icterus spurius*),
  compared with Baltimore oriole,
  85, 86.
Otter, 160, 161.

Peacock, 54.
Petrifaction and putrefaction, 3.

INDEX

INDEX